D1153930

The Least Likely to Succeed

Jack Clifford

Creator of the Food Network

By Jack Clifford

with Rich Wolfe

Published by Lone Wolfe Press, a division of Richcraft. Distribution and marketing by Wolfegang Marketing Systems, Ltd.

Layout: Dave Reed

Author's agent: T. Roy Gaul

Rich Wolfe can be reached at 602-738-5889

ISBN: 978-0-9963247-5-5

Printed in the United States

DEDICATION

To my wonderful, wonderful sister

Dr. Rosejean Clifford Hinsdale

My mentor, my cheerleader, my catalyst, my compass!

Contents

Foreword

ROBIN LEACH

Robin Leach

Jack was the baldheaded bullet of the newspaper business, a remarkable man who took a kernel of an idea and turned it into a giant hit television network. He was smart enough to know that he needed somebody who understood both journalism and television programming and production. He hired Reese Schonfeld, who was the guy Ted Turner turned to to build CNN.

Jack, being a smart businessman, hired the best. How does a man who's living in Rhode Island get to be so big in one of the toughest businesses around? It was because he had the uncanny knack and belief in going out on a limb and hiring the best that money could buy and letting them run with a project. Reese Schonfeld, on a very tight budget, got the Food Network off the ground, and, as far as I know, never had a problem with anything he wanted when he asked Jack Clifford for it.

The two of them made what then was an unbelievable deal with me. Jack Clifford, like Rupert Murdoch, had this—I don't know whether it's something that's just ingrained in you by Mother Nature or what—but this will to succeed. His personality was such that you didn't go against him. You went with him. You knew he was the captain of the ship, and you wanted him to sail into port and get applause.

He was quite remarkable in his enthusiasm and support. It was never a concern on his part. It was never a competition, never a confrontation. It was always, "Do you have enough to do what you say you can do?"

You know, they let me go off around the country, talking to cable affiliates to carry this remarkable creation called the Television Food Network. What Jack did when he got to the cable TV conventions was prove that he was a chief corporate officer who really ran and understood the business he was developing and building.

We might have had the razzle-dazzle of show business in the way we got the network up and running, but he was the—I won't say the crazy glue—certainly the glue that proved to the television operators that the ProJo Company and ProJo Communications was more than 100 percent behind the idea of the Television Food Network. The Food Network did not come from anybody on Madison Avenue. It did not come from television executives in sharkskin suits in Los Angeles. It came from Providence, Rhode Island.

Joe Langhan was Jack's rep in all of our insanity in New York. Joe watched the pennies because if you don't watch the pennies, you don't get the pounds, as we say in England. Joe was very serious about the mission at hand. He ensured that the ship sailed into harbor without getting stuck on a sandbank.

When Reese came to me with the idea, I thought in the back of my mind that it was insanity. But, one, Reese is a very convincing man, and, two, you have to remember that I worked for him at CNN. If you thought you could have built a news network with elastic bands and chewing gum, you would have laughed at that, too. But you knew that he was so serious, he was going to pull it off, and he would give you whatever support was needed.

I had several famous chefs on *Lifestyles*. I felt that celebrity chefs were becoming akin to rock stars in the music world. There was as much interest in guys like Emeril Lagasse or Wolfgang Puck as there was for Rod Stewart or Mick Jagger. I thought that if it was presented properly, they could build a successful cable network out of it.

The great thing about Clifford is that he's a man of the salt, as we say in England. He was as equal and as ordinary as the guy who swept the studio of the star chefs we were booking. He got on with everybody.

I do remember two things. The first night we launched at that studio on 39th Street and 10th Avenue, you couldn't have found a cheaper television studio in the world to start a network from. There were hookers on a snowy night huddled in the front entrance of the building that led to our studio. I always remember joking with Jack that this was no way for anybody to come to work walking through a street standing brothel. He laughed and said, "It's the show that comes out of the TV cameras that makes it work."

I remember that first night we did the show there were two rats or maybe very big mice. The rodents ran across the floor of the studio, live during the show. I was so bemused and shocked by it I asked the cameraman live to turn his camera on the two little pests scurrying across the floor. I realized afterward that that probably was something I shouldn't have done. I remember half apologizing the next day to Joe and Jack, and Reese intervened and said, "Great television. People saw we were live" and gave no reprimand.

I remember the first sales trip we all made together was to a cable TV convention at the Moscone Convention Center in San Francisco. I was always the one banging the drums to say, "We have to prove to the cable operators that we have the money to stay in business for a year." I was trying to tell Jack and Reese that perception of our longevity to come was based on our initial splash.

I can't remember the outcome of it all, but I do remember all of us, after we made whatever that original splash was, walking down the streets of San Francisco, and Jack Clifford said to me, "You sure know how to spend somebody else's money."

I loved him. He was a unique father figure from the business side. Jack left Reese and Joe to do the programming. Jack was there to make sure it happened. You have to remember that when the Food Network launched, it was an unbelievable undertaking. It had never been done before quite that way. You could look back at it five years after the fact and still be amazed at what was pulled off by a unique team of people. I mean, Jack Clifford was not show business splash. He was, and I say this with love and affection, if you asked Central Casting to give you an accountant—a smart, serious businessman from Providence, Rhode Island—they would have probably bought you Jack Clifford.

I was always fun to work with because I thought we always had to project. I mean, how many ways can you show how to cook roast beef on television? That was the worry I had when they originally came to me and when I went and met the team.

Someone said, "What's the highest-rated television show in the world?" I didn't have a clue. I thought he was talking about *Dallas*, the prime-time soap opera. I couldn't even think what he was talking about. The Super Bowl in those days didn't have 114 million viewers. He said to me, "It's the Yule Log on Christmas Eve." It's true to this day. Everybody turns it on on Christmas Eve. That was his answer to my concern about how many times you could see roast beef being cut. How many times do you see flames flicking over wood?

It was a great team of people, and that again was attributable to Jack Clifford. He built a formidable television team out of a number of people who'd never been "deeply involved" with television before. You couldn't have asked for a better leader.

The Least Likely to Succeed

Jack Clifford
Creator of the
Food Network

Rich Wolfe

Chapter 1

Sweet Home Grand Rapids

Certificate of honorable mention, 1934 photograph contest, one year old.

Rich Wolfe

One foot in childhood, one foot in adulthood

The early fall of 1933 saw the Great Depression hit its lowest point. Franklin Roosevelt was firmly in the White House, and the New Deal was underway. Hitler and Nazi Germany were threatening to overrun Europe. The "Steel City" of Gary, Indiana, was a center of American industrialization. My parents, Jack and Pauline Arndt Clifford, were awaiting the birth of their second child. Jack was disturbed by this in that the family certainly did not need a second youngster to feed. However, the first Clifford child, Rosejean, age eleven, was thrilled at the prospect of having a sibling, and she prayed each night that a boy would be joining the family. Jack worked for the Pennsylvania Railroad as a policeman. America's railroads were a nation unto themselves because most of the nation's cargo and passenger transportation was handled by train until the late 1950s. The railroad police had jurisdiction over all crime committed on railroad property. The railroads still provide the largest land-based cargo service to this day, but passenger service is now the airlines' business. In any case, Jack worked and lived in Gary where much of the nation's steel was produced and shipped by train.

Little Rosejean's prayers were answered at 7:00 a.m. on September 13, 1933, with the birth of her baby brother Jack Carl Clifford. That's me! The middle name given me was after my uncle Carl Arndt. I grew to deeply love him and his wife, my aunt Dorothy. During summers in high school I worked on Carl's farms. My aunt was one of the world's greatest cooks. Those 5 a.m. breakfasts on the farm were spectacular. I grew to be over six feet tall by the time I was fourteen. Thanks to the summer farm work, I was quite strong, so that fall I went out for football and in the spring baseball. I was a good long-ball hitter and batted cleanup. Being a two hundred pounder I played center on offense and inside linebacker on defense for the football team. My family could not afford the needed money for college for my sister or me. My sister wanted me to attend college, but my interests were sports and theater and my grades were a low C. My sister and I attended a public high school, and neither of us fit in. In spite of the many sports achievements and the number of theatrical performances I was in, I was ignored socially and left out of most school events. Like so many youngsters, I turned to humor and comedy and became a class cutup. This did not sit well with the faculty! The tide was about to turn!

In the spring semester of my sophomore year I met a guy who loved theater. His name was Bob Gray, and he was incredible. He convinced me I could be an actor, and together we produced the school pep rallies staring yours truly. They were very funny and poked fun at coaches and the eccentric classroom teachers.

That summer Bob and I found a friend whose father owned an 8mm home movie camera. It was a single 8 and preceded Kodak's development of double 8mm home film cameras. We wrote a script and recruited a cast. Each person who joined us had to put $2.50 in to defray the cost of production. We made our movie, *The Curse of Ackenaldo*. It ran fifteen minutes, and I played the Ackenaldo Monster. We had no sound. We learned a great deal about film production, so that fall we made a second movie called *The Sign of the Beast* that ran thirty minutes. It was our masterpiece. Bob and I decided to show our films at the high school auditorium and sold tickets for ten cents apiece. We had a sellout; the entire student body of 1,100 attended. The cast of the movies gathered backstage with various sound effects, a microphone, and a phonograph to add dramatic musical background. Believe it or not it worked. We established a movie production club at the school called the Flicker Club, and the school librarian Mrs. Kriminsky gladly became our faculty sponsor. This was twenty-five years before Steven Spielberg did the same thing only better.

My sister is eleven years older than I am, and from the time she can remember, she wanted a baby brother. My mother, unfortunately, had a heart condition, and the doctor told her when she gave birth to my sister that she should not have any more children. In September 1933 yours truly appeared on the scene. My sister was delighted and has always treated me with very special care and consideration. She has been wonderful to me.

When I was four years old, she decided she was going to teach me to read. My sister went on to an almost forty-year teaching career all the way from high school to the college level, but she started out at fifteen teaching her younger brother to read. By the time I got to kindergarten, I could read. I certainly could not read the encyclopedia, but I could read kids' stories. The teacher recognized this and decided to let me read the children's story every day for a while that came after we had our little nap. Therefore, I probably never developed a problem with stage fright. I just got up and read the story. I must have been okay because the kids never complained. My sister Rosejean started an avalanche of opportunities for me.

My sister and mentor, Rosejean Clifford Hinsdale, 2009.

From as far back as I can remember, I listened to radio. Like kids watch TV today, I listened to the radio. We had wonderful shows, such as *Superman, Mr. District Attorney, Pursuit, Inner Sanctum, The Shadow, The Lone Ranger, Gangbusters, Boston Blackie,* and of course *Dragnet,* which started on radio and then transferred over to TV, as did *Gunsmoke. Gunsmoke* started on radio, but the guy playing the leading man with a deep baritone voice was a short, little, fat man so he could not get the job on television. When *Gunsmoke* went on TV, the lead was played by a big hunk named James Arness. Anyway, transference took place during the 50s, the exciting age of new programming on television.

Early on we moved from Gary, Indiana, to Grand Rapids, Michigan. Chuck DeShane was a football player for the Detroit Lions. He was from Grand Rapids, Michigan, a great, big, powerful guy, nice fellow. In those days, football players didn't get paid very much. They really played for the love of the game more than anything else. It was roughly a few thousand dollars. My father was the head of a police crew, he was in charge of the division, and Chuck would work for him in the off-season. I would go down to my father's office, and Chuck would be out there working. He was a massive guy, stood about six feet, six inches, probably 280 pounds.

Oh, he was a big guy but a very sweet guy, very kind. He was very nice to me. My father and I wanted badly to see Chuck play football. So, I went out and got an extra job and did all kinds of things to save up $100 to get a TV so we could watch Chuck play! I bought a GE seventeen-inch black and white TV. The console was fake wood.

My dad was thrilled. He was very proud that I was able to do this. We hooked it up downstairs and I got up on the roof. I wiggled the wire through some cracks and finally got the antenna up on the roof. I was turning it and turning it, and Dad said, "You got it. I can see the picture fine." So I went downstairs and started watching our TV.

The signal from Detroit was not very good. I should have known better, but all you could see was a snowy screen and occasionally players going by. If I saw his number, I felt satisfied. That taught me another lesson: it is what's on the feed that is important. The feed isn't important. A lot of people don't figure that out. In my business in radio and television, they thought the technology was more important than what they were doing.

A Play-tonic Relationship

TOM CARLSON

Tom Carlson and Jack Clifford are lifelong friends. Carlson is a charter member of the Wierenga Scholarship Committee for Ottawa Hills High School, which they both attended. He is the founder of Naco Wellness Initiative, which promotes wellness and disease prevention in the borderland region of Naco, Arizona.

Tom Carlson

I loved Jack dearly as a brother. We can finish each other's sentences. We played together daily and did all the things kids do when they're growing up. We would argue over who was going to pull who in the red wagon and who was going to be first on the sled down the hill.

Jack had a dog named King, a German shepherd. We'd get King to pull the sled and the wagon. Those were good times.

I'd go out down the road and just say, "Mom, I'm going over to Jackie's to play for a while."

"Okay, well, be home for supper."

I'd walk out, and that would be the end of it. Our parents weren't concerned about safety or security or anything like that. It was a very open town. There wasn't a lot of traffic. We never had safety issues. We could just concentrate on the fun. We had a gang of kids we played with. We played Kick the Can out on the street.

Jack loved to tell a joke and loved to be mischievous. We made a little shack in his backyard where we would invite the kids in to do secret things and have secret hand signals and be part of the club. Jack had a gift for making you laugh. That always came through. He wanted to do fun things.

We would play sandlot baseball. That was back when we'd have pickup teams. We'd be about nine or ten. We were interested in baseball and other sports. There wasn't any organized stuff in those days. We'd go to Franklin Park, a couple of blocks away, a big park. We'd make a baseball diamond out of the rocks. There weren't any bases. We'd go find two big rocks and put them there. Jack loved baseball. He absolutely was just taken with it. He was on the clumsy side. He didn't go smoothly, but boy could he hit that ball.

We got into trouble together all the time. We used to go into other people's gardens and pick the fruit. There wasn't any theft involved or things like that. You'd do water balloons and throw them on the porches, and you could do tricks at Halloween and raise hell.

There was nothing destructive or serious. It was fun things. At

Tom Carlson (left), my childhood friend since age three, in Grand Rapids, Michigan. We remain close friends to this day. Now and at nine years old in 1942.

that time, you loved to do things to get the neighbor's goat, to ring the doorbell and run away, simple things like that.

We never got into any big trouble. There was certainly never any police involved. Later on in high school, we did crazy things. We made a yo-yo with a terribly long string and went up to the fifth floor of the school building and were trying to make it work outside the window. We didn't get it to work very well. Just fun stuff.

Jack used to love to make strange noises and get people to laugh at him. The kids thought that was great. He was an impersonator in that way. I remember sitting in class one time—this was springtime, and the windows were open. He started making these crazy noises, and the principal was walking by outside. He walked in the room and said, "Who did that? Who did that?" I don't remember if Jack fessed up or not.

Jack has always loved an audience. In high school, he was really good on stage with jokes. He had a string of jokes. We had these pep rallies before football games on Fridays. The whole school would show up in the auditorium. Somebody in the drama club pushed Jack out on the stage one time and said, "Tell your jokes out there," and he did. He kept getting such great reactions that he started loving doing it, and he was good at it. He was really good. It was very unusual for a kid to go out on stage and do humorous things. He was the only one who'd do that.

We had a movie club in high school where he got the folks together. We'd cut little stories about the ghost of Frankenstein and the werewolf and all that stuff. We would make silent movies on the old eight millimeters and show them, try to make a little money. We'd sit in the front row and holler out the scripts. Jack was always the leader in that sort of thing. We'd charge ten cents.

He wasn't a ladies' man in high school. That happened in college. We kept in touch during college. After college, we lost touch for a very long time. He moved to Arizona.

Jack has got a way of sticking with stuff until he gets it the way he wants it. I would almost call him a perfectionist. He would talk me into going over to a local elementary school property to pitch him tennis balls. You couldn't use a baseball over there. We did this for hours. He really learned to get a batting eye that way. That is what led him to be such a good hitter.

He eventually went to high school sports, but baseball is what he excelled in. He knocked the cover off a ball. I mean, the guy could hit. He was an outfielder and said he hoped the ball wouldn't come to him in center field because he couldn't run that fast.

I still remember one home run. There was a ballpark in Grand Rapids on top of a big reservoir. It had a big ball diamond on it. He hit that ball out of the park. That's his home run of a lifetime! He would say that kind of experience was what really gave him a lot of confidence.

My high school class picture, age seventeen, May 1951.

Our parents would take us down to the Detroit Tigers games. Ted Spoelstra's dad would pile us all in the car, and we'd go down to see a Tigers game, which we thought was really over the top.

Baseball certainly made Jack feel good about himself. In high school, toward the end there, a few of us were playing ball over in the park, another pickup game with the rock bases. This one kid, Jack Neal, was on the high school team. He was a pretty good pitcher. A few of our classmate girls showed up and started watching. This guy was going to show them how good a pitcher he was.

Jack was standing at the plate. He threw Jack a high fastball, and Jack knocked it a mile. This poor pitcher, he didn't talk to Jack for a long time after that.

We had favorite Tigers players. Hal Newhouser and Dizzy Trout were star pitchers. Both were twenty-game winners. George Kell was the third baseman. At the time, we knew them all. I remember when Frank House was signed for a $75,000 bonus. That was considered astronomical, and he didn't make the grade either.

The scholarship fund at our Grand Rapids high school that Jack set up a few years ago is just an incredible legacy to leave behind when you consider all the kids who benefited. For me, it means a lot because it went back to our high school. He's given a lot of money and helped a lot of folks go forward. For me, that legacy just keeps on moving. It's now up to twenty or thirty graduates.

I was surprised at how well he did. As a friend, we had a strong bond. His stick-to-itiveness got him there. He's tenacious. He taught himself to do all the right things, and he became fortunate in some of his connections and contacts as well. He took advantage of them. He created his own opportunities and did something with them. I was delighted for him, and I still am, of course. But, as a close friend, I don't think about the money. I just don't. We just get together and have a good time.

There's No Expiration Date on Dreams

RUTH BISHOP

Ruth Bishop

Since joining the Grand Rapids Community Foundation in 1992, Ruth has administered a variety of education-related programs. She is responsible for administering over eighty scholarship funds providing a total of $1 million each year and supports local efforts targeting college access for all. She is the program director for the Youth Enrichment Scholarship (YES) program, a financial aid program providing scholarships to students beginning in the fourth grade for summer activities and culminating in a scholarship for college or vocational training upon successful completion of high school.

I know Jack through the Grand Rapids Community Foundation because he established a scholarship in honor of his high school principal. We administer that scholarship.

I first started talking with Jack back in 2001, when he had gotten together with a few of his high school buddies he graduated with at Ottawa Hills High School. He had been thinking about his high school principal, Elmo Wierenga, who really played a big part in Jack's life. Jack came from a middle-class working family. At the time, back in the forties, his parents weren't particularly interested in or didn't encourage him to go on to any higher education. Not that they didn't believe in it, but they didn't have the money or whatever.

Elmo Wierenga, the principal at Ottawa Hills, took a liking to Jack, saw potential in him. Jack admits that he was actually voted "the least likely to succeed" by his graduation classmates. Jack wasn't a great student and just flew under the radar, but the principal really saw potential in him. He said, "Jack, I really want you to consider going to college."

Jack thought Elmo had been the spark behind his decision to go to college. He went to community college here in Grand Rapids and then transferred to Western Michigan.

Jack wanted to honor this principal. The principal at that point was still alive, but he was ailing and not doing well. Jack did actually have a chance to talk with him before he died, and then he talked with the family members after that.

Ottawa Hills has this incredible history of people who have graduated and gone on to do just incredible things but also have a real deep loyalty to the school.

Jack gave a substantial amount of money to start the scholarship fund. Then there was an alumni group here in Grand Rapids that also was doing some scholarship work. They decided to merge their money, and all the money was put here in the Grand Rapids Community Foundation. We administer over eighty scholarship funds.

Jack really wanted to be involved in this. Once the criteria were established, he wanted to make sure the scholarship focused on the type of student Jack was, the type who might not necessarily be at the top of their class, might not be the top scholar. Jack wanted to find the student who showed promise and was eager, so he could just give the additional encouragement Elmo Wierenga had given him.

The committee gets together every year. It's a hoot for me to coordinate the scholarship selection process because it's like a reunion every time they get back together. We have other people from the community on the selection committee, and there are a few representatives from the alumni group who take part. Jack flies back in every year for the meeting. I've been working with him on the scholarship since 2002, and it's just an incredible time to see them get together. Jack is such a successful person. He just puts everybody at ease; everyone feels comfortable around him.

We do interviews for the scholarship. We select six high school seniors whom we then interview in one day. When we go through that interview process, Jack is the most nurturing, encouraging person as we talk with these students. He just totally puts them at ease.

I was a little concerned, honestly, about having them go through an interview process. A lot of these students have experienced disappointments in their life, and to bring them in for an interview and then not have every one of them receive the scholarship, I was concerned about just another disappointment.

Even though all the students have to interview, not every one of them receives a scholarship. Jack is always so encouraging to them that I know they all leave with a sense of positivity toward their future. The interview process is actually a positive thing because they all get to meet Jack.

One of the original recipients went on to graduate from college and is now working here in Grand Rapids. She is now one of the selection committee members. That brings some youth to the committee as well, and the students can relate to her. That's a great thing.

Jack had asked me one year about one of the original recipients who received the scholarship. "What happened? Have you heard anything more from this particular student?"

I located her, and she was living in Prescott, Arizona. She was married with a couple of kids and is now working at a resident home for young women who need special education attention.

Jack and Beverly connected with her, and they went out to dinner together. Jack was just thrilled, just absolutely thrilled, and he had a chance to hear more about her life and then to meet her kids. He's just such a likable, easily approachable, warm, and open person.

Reminiscing: Former Ottawa Hills boys basketball coach Bob Hendrickson, here with wife Joan, has plenty of awards and keepsakes to remind him of the school's success. Ottawa Hills will rename its gym after Hendrickson in a ceremony Friday evening.

Call him 'coach'

Bob Hendrickson: Lifelong friend who was a childhood friend and fellow student at Ottawa Hills. Bob went on to become a teacher, coach and principal at the school. He also sits on the foundation board with me at the Elmo Wierenga Scholarship.

Rich Wolfe

Chapter 2

WMU – I Saw It on the Radio

**Graduating from Western Michigan University,
with my parents Pauline and Jack Charles Clifford, 1956.**

Rich Wolfe

The Boy Wonder Had the Boys Wondering

I graduated from college in January 1956. While in college, I got involved in building an on-campus radio station that was wired into the dormitories; it was not transmitted over the air, so we were not required to have FCC licensing. We didn't have the money to buy a transmitter anyway. It went from the studio to the transmitter just like any other radio station. Then the audio was transmitted on a wire just as with most cable TV. It went into the power supply of various dormitories, and any radio plugged into the wall could pick up the signal. It didn't interfere with any other signal; it just picked up that one if you wanted it. Therefore, we had a nice built-in audience. I was very active with that and thought it was a lot of fun. It got me going as to what I wanted to do for a living. One day I decided to take a class on radio production because the university had an FM radio station. Keep in mind this was the early 50s and FM was just beginning. There were very few FM sets. It was slow to begin, but then eventually, of course, it took over. National Public Radio was not operating, so we had to create our own programs. Most of them were lectures by professors, and the kids could make up some classwork by listening to the radio station. In any case, I decided to take a class in radio production so I could be more useful at the little radio station we built. It turned out we used the defunct agricultural farm at Western Michigan University. The only thing left for us was the chicken house, so that's where we built. We cleaned it up and painted it.

We made it at least reasonably presentable. We had a board for turning on microphones and turning off records like a regular radio station. Eventually, we even had our own newswire service from what was then called College Radio Corporation. They presented us with a teletype and paper and ribbons and periodically would refill those for us. We would do a newscast every evening. It was sponsored by Lucky Strike cigarettes. Cigarettes were very popular in those days.

Since we now had our own radio station, we could learn some things we could not learn elsewhere. I became the general manager after there was a falling out with a kid who originally designed the radio operation. I don't know what happened, but they asked me to take it over, and I did. I looked older—I was balding even at nineteen—and so they said, you do it. I took this course, and the professor thought I was older than the other kids. He guessed I was in my thirties. One day, he wrote on the blackboard that he was not going to be in for class but that Jack Clifford would run the class. He never asked me to do it; he just did it. It was fun and everybody was happy.

One day I was worried about where I was going to get another job that could help support my meager income so I could pay for my education. I had sent everybody on after class was over, closed the door, and started to walk into the hall when I was stopped by a guy in a business suit by the name of Chuck Mefford. He was the program director at WKMI Radio. AM ruled the radio world then and television was just beginning. He asked me, "Professor, do you have anybody here, one of your students, who can do an all-night, brand-new disc jockey program?" I said, "How much does it pay?" He said, "$1 an hour," which in those days was not great but was not bad. I told him I had one student. "Who is it?" he asked. I said, "Me!" He said, "Wait, you're the professor." I said, "No I'm not. I am just helping out, and he uses me as his assistant." He said, "Well, come on down to the radio station tonight and talk to Jeff Lane, who is our guy on the air." What I didn't know was that Jeff was doing both early evening and late night and was getting damn tired of it. I said, "Okay, I'll be down there. What time?" He said, "Get there at about a quarter to eight."

It was within walking distance of the off-campus apartment where I lived with four other guys. I walked on down to the State Theatre where the radio station was located on the top floor of the three-story building. I went up the fire escape as instructed, and there Jeff Lane had the door of the studio wedged open with a wood block. I kicked the wood block out of the way and closed the door behind me. The only person in there was Jeff. He was on the air and running the whole show, because everybody else had gone home. He waved me into the control room. I went in, and as he played a record, he turned to me and said, "Are you Clifford?" And I said, "Yup." He said, "Here's what we're going to do. In about two or three minutes, I am going out to get a newscast off the wire." In those days, they provided five-minute capsule newscasts from Associated Press or United Press. He said, "I am going to get a five-minute newscast. I will come back in and do the news, and then at 8:00, you're going on the air." I said, "Okay, I am going on the air?" I sort of looked puzzled, and he said, "Yeah, you have been hired." I said, "I have?" He said, "Yeah, yeah, you're hired. Just calm down." And I said, "Okay, whatever you say, Jeff." He said, "I am going to put a long record on so I can go out there and get the news. I'll come back, and after that record ends, I'll do a commercial, and after that, I'll do the newscast, and then at 8:00, I'll give you the mike." So, I said, "Okay." He did what he said he was going to do. Then he got out of the chair next to the microphone and put me in it. He said, "Now, great news, ladies and gentlemen, boys and girls," and was laughing to himself. He said, "We've got a new DJ here. He is a good-looking college student over at Western Michigan, and he is big and handsome, and his name is Clifford, and we are going to call his show *Cruising with Clifford*." So I got labeled with that.

As a matter of fact, I go back every year—I am on the Communication School Board at my university. People still remember *Cruising with Clifford*, believe it or not. Not many, but a few. Anyhow, I went on the air at 8:00 and I have been, in one way or another, on the air ever since.

And it helped with the girls. I mean, I was in Kalamazoo, Michigan. I was a celebrity. They didn't have any other celebrities. They didn't have a Major League Baseball team or anything. They had some college athletes who were well known. Plus, Kalamazoo's own hero, Derek Jeter, hadn't been born yet. I certainly had a wonderful time with the ladies and with my studies, and I did well. The girls all wanted to come down to the studio, and I couldn't let them do that. I would have been fired instantaneously. I was a straight shooter. I didn't mess with them at all; I just got a lot of dates, but nothing serious. I took my job very seriously. I really enjoyed being on the air.

I never swore nor said *dammit* or *hell* or anything like that on the air. At the radio station in Kalamazoo, the program director would have a staff meeting with the announcers. We would talk about how we approached our shows. One of the guys on the air made the classic blunder. He was supposed to say, "That reminds me to tell you folks that for donuts around the clock, it's Jake's Delights Donut Shop." But he said, "That reminds me to tell you folks that for donuts around the *cock*, it's Jake's Delights Donut Shop." Nothing happened, but he thought he was going to be finished.

I was on all night, and the policy was that the DJ on board had to talk at the end of each record because they wanted to train the audience to expect to hear a human voice. Hopefully that human voice would be reading a commercial, and the station would get paid more, so I had to talk between each record. I had to come up with material from anything I could dream up—magazines, newspapers, books.

The radio station discovered that I had played high school football and baseball, and they wanted me to do their sports. So I started doing that at WMCR, which was the FM station on campus. They hired me to do the university's sports. I did a play-by-play of their football, basketball, and baseball. WMU was very good at baseball. They had gone to the College World Series of Baseball a couple of times. The last year they went they almost won. They lost in the last game. I have a plaque they gave to me just recently at a party in Kalamazoo for the team that year. The team insisted I be part of that party, although I never played; I just broadcasted the games. They gave me a Western Michigan baseball cap, and on the team photo, the guys had reserved a spot for me. That picture hangs proudly on my wall today.

I fell in love with radio. It was fun, I was completely in command, and I was the only one at the station from about 8:00 at night until 5:30 in the morning. I did everything: weather, sports, and news. I was young and energetic and just absolutely had a wonderful time.

They had a dial-up transmitter system that was like a telephone. Every hour on the hour I had to do a transmitter reading. If anything went haywire, I would have to call Ken, our engineer at home. Ken would head in there and come marching out with a fixed transmitter. That only happened once or twice.

One night while I was on the air I saw on the wire service that people were beginning to see tornados in parts of Michigan.

People hadn't seen one in years, and one was headed toward our general region. I quickly got on the phone with the weather service. They said it was very serious. WKZO, our competitor, was off the air at that time, as this was 1:00 in the morning. I thought, *I have to do this, I have to warn people.* I checked the AP and the UP wire, and there was the tornado information. I called Ken, the engineer, and said, "You better get down here because I am going to go out of format and start doing coverage of these tornados to help people know where they are, because the other radio station that serves the market isn't on the air to do it." Ken came down. He ran the board while I did all of the running around the studio getting all the wire service material. I did something that hadn't been done before. I put the weather bureau on the radio. I put them on over our telephone so they could broadcast on our signal to talk about the weather. I would ask questions and they would give me the answers. We were on the air. It was quite a thing. It hadn't been done before as far as I know, and it was one of the very early uses of that.

I went on all night until the DJ and replacement came in, and by this time the tornados had passed. There was some destruction but fortunately not much. I went home dead tired that Saturday morning. I worked that afternoon, and Sunday afternoon I was "riding the board" as they say, while we carried sports events from the network. Monday, I went in for my usual shift, which began at 3:00, and was called to the general manager's office. His name was Bud Popke. Bud said to me, "Jack, you were out of format on Friday night on that tornado stuff." I thought he was going to bawl me out for going out of format, and he said, "That was a damn smart thing you did." I said, "Well, thank you." He said, "Look over in the corner." There were bags of telegrams congratulating our radio station for doing tornado alerts.

That really made my day at the Kalamazoo radio station. I got letter upon letter. People would stop me to thank me because I probably saved a few lives and didn't know it. That was a big moment. Two things happened: I got a raise, but more importantly, I became aware of the importance of public broadcasting. You didn't have to wait until tomorrow to find out what was happening tonight; you heard about it now. It was important to hear about it now. Not just the score of the baseball game but whether a tornado might be bearing down on your town, or whether it was another weather crisis, or a war had broken out, or whatever it was. Radio was there and events could be instantaneously reported. That taught me a lesson. From that point forward, if I was going to stay in radio or broadcasting, I believed in community service. I built my career in radio and television on the premise that the news we did was the most important programming we could do, more important than the game shows and the comedy hours. The latter is entertainment and is important, but the news and how it is presented is the most important. That all began at that moment by recognizing that not only did I make the right decision, I did it the right way and I helped people.

When I was in high school, television came to Grand Rapids in the form of WOOD Channel 8, an NBC affiliate. The CBS affiliate was WKZO in Kalamazoo. My father was actually most impressed with television. Later in his life, he couldn't believe his son was coming flying through the air in the living room. My father was born in 1889, so he saw the car invented, the radio debut, and airplanes come about, but he really was impressed with the fact that I was on television.

The first time I ever saw television was in Grand Rapids. We lived around the corner and down the street from a bar. They had a sign that said SEE TV HERE in order to draw people into the bar where they could watch some television. Of course, I couldn't go into a bar—I was just a kid—so I would stare through the window and try to see it. I saw media spheres moving across the screen. I really got entranced by it when I visited my uncle in Gary, Indiana, when I was about twelve. He had a Philco TV with a six- to seven-inch screen. He had a water magnifier, a big tank of water in front of it, that made it into more like a twelve-inch TV. The Chicago High School Championship football game at Soldier Field was on TV, in black and white of course (all TVs were black and white).

I sat there mystified. I could not believe I was seeing a football game on the television set. To me, it was like the face of God. I was thunderstruck. From that moment on, I was determined to do something in broadcasting, which eventually led to WKMI in my college years, helping pay my way through college. I graduated from college in January 1956. It took me four and a half years to get through because I was working. I got my degree in communications.

In the summers during college, I worked wherever I could. I worked at a hamburger place frying hamburgers and making french fries, and I managed it at night. It was the best hamburger joint. I had the blessing in one sense of being big, and I looked so much older because I was balding. Ma and Pa Burns owned the restaurant. I closed the place at 11 p.m. each night. They made wonderful chili. It was my job to take the double boiler with the leftover chili and put it in the freezer. The next morning Pa thawed out the chili and made a whole new batch on top of the leftover chili and put it back on the burner to cook. The whole time I worked there I don't think the pot was ever cleaned.

I graduated from college in January, and the next September, my twenty-second birthday, I was drafted. We had just gotten out of the Korean War and we still had a peacetime army, so I was drafted. I knew this was coming but didn't know when. I had to go to the general manager at the station and tell him I was drafted and would be leaving in a couple of weeks. He went bananas. He said, "How old are you?" I told him I was only twenty-two. He said, "My God! We thought you were thirty-five years old!" I said, 'Well, you never asked me and I never told you." He said, "Well, you son of a . . ." then, "okay, I understand."

So, I went off to my service duties. I had played high school football and had hurt my leg badly, my right leg, and had broken my knee, which was full of chips. I went through a whole day at Fort Wayne, not Fort Wayne, Indiana, but Fort Wayne in Detroit, Michigan, where they did the preinduction physicals for the army. Hundreds of guys were naked all day running around, checking this and checking that. It was a terrible experience. It was cold as hell there. This was in September. My name was called along with four or five other guys toward the end of the day. We had to go into a room and do exercises because they were worried about our knees. I got dressed and ready to get into the lines for the buses taking us to the railroad station so we could catch the train to Fort Leonard Wood, Missouri, for our basic training.

As I was stepping up onto the bus, I heard my name and number called. Someone said, "Please report to the major's office." I thought, *What the hell happened? What could have possibly happened?* I had made friends with all of these guys around me, and now I was going to get on the bus with people I didn't know. I was a little frightened of the whole thing anyway. I went off to the major's office. I walked up there, and a guy motioned me to come in. I said, "I am recruit Clifford." He said, "Oh, sorry, I got bad news for you. You are never going to serve in this man's army." I said, "Well, what have I done?" He said, "Your leg is too difficult for us to repair and you are being reclassified 4F." I was secretly happy! I didn't know if I should kiss him or sing the national anthem. I stood up, and he said, "Are you all right, son?" I said, "Yeah, yeah I am." He gave me a bus token and a ticket for a hamburger at some place, because it was about a three-hour drive to Grand Rapids. I was so dumbstruck; it was almost like a fellow who was told he's going to walk the last walk. They sit you in the chair, and then they say, "You're free to go." I couldn't believe this was happening to me! I called the radio station the next day, and they said, "Well, come on back to work." I went back on the air, and nothing was ever said about it, and away we went from there. Finally, when I turned about forty, I got my knee fixed.

Back at Kalamazoo I broadcast baseball and football for WMCR, the college radio station. It is now called WMUK—terrible call letters—for Western Michigan University, Kalamazoo, an FM station. WMCR was Western Michigan College Radio. I did the ball games and had a lot of fun. I have been very active in the communication school there.

AAA, the American Automobile Association, ran ads on all Michigan radio stations. They would make reference to locations in Detroit. They did not want to do one slanted toward Kalamazoo. I read the Kalamazoo commercial while listening to the Detroit commercial so that I could get my commercial in at the same pace as the guy in Detroit. The words were almost the same but not quite. It was very difficult to do, trying to focus on two things— read the commercial right and also get it done.

When the announcer said, "For AAA, call 555-1212," I was saying the same thing, except the phone number was different, and bingo, I would hit the switch and we're back to the network. I never made a mistake on that one. It was very interesting. Radio was a great deal of fun.

One day, I must have dozed off. I was still working seven days per week. All of a sudden I heard that cue and I thought, *Oh my gosh,*

I've got to do something! So, I dashed through the double doors, through the adjacent production studio, to the teletype, tripped and fell, and slid under the teletype machine and knocked myself out. The next thing I know, I'm being shaken by the general manager who was pulling me out from under the machine. They forgave me, but boy, did that scare me.

The most interesting aspect off the air in Kalamazoo was the fact that I became a local celebrity. We were the only thing on there. *Cruising with Clifford* was beamed all over Kalamazoo and Battle Creek. It brought enormous pressure on me from women. I got many dozens of phone calls from lonely women. I had to answer the phone because I was the only one at the station. I ran everything from 8:00 at night until 5:30 the following morning. I answered the phone, "WKMI, how may I help you?" These women were aggressive as hell, and I was raised in a very, shall we say, conservative family. I was dumbfounded. I didn't know what to say to these women. Wisely, looking back, I never took advantage of the options provided. They were incredible. But that was radio.

One interesting sidebar. I did a lot of fraternity, sorority, and high school sock hops. I actually was paid more by these people than at the station. I made $100 a night back in 1954 . . . enormous money at that time.

I had a car, and most guys didn't in those days. I was having a heck of a good life. The only problem was I never slept! I was tired a lot because I worked all night and went to school all day. I thought I was a pretty sharp guy. I was dating a nurse because she worked the same hours I worked.

She had Sunday night off, so we would go out then to a movie or something. She was a nice girl. I got up the energy to put my arm around her in the motion picture theater, a fast-moving character like myself. I loved those hard licorice nibs. So I am cuddling up, when I bit down on that licorice and cracked a tooth. I screamed! She thought I'd had a heart attack! I said, "No, I'm all right, just a little sore here." I went to the dentist the next morning. He said, "I can't save that tooth. We are going to have to pull it." That is the only tooth I've ever lost. He got me an appointment with a dental surgeon in the same building to pull this tooth. I could hardly wait. He gave me some painkiller, which helped a bit, but it was really terrible. I could hardly eat anything, just drink. I went to the office of the dental surgeon the next day, and I noticed that his receptionist was one of the most stunning young women I had ever seen, absolutely gorgeous, and very pleasant. I'm this big-time radio announcer, you gotta remember. I got to be a pretty hot shot. I am bragging to her about all of the wonderful stars I had interviewed. She was doing her best to ignore me. She had to assist the dentist in this whole process, "Open your mouth, close your mouth, etc." The surgeon says they are going to have to numb me. He gave me a shot of Novocaine, as I was talking to her and saying how I met Perry Como.

For those days, that was really big! I wanted her to know how important I was. All of a sudden I cannot say a word. The dentist had his back to me, and I could tell he was laughing. He says, "Sounds like he is pretty numb there, huh?" She is chuckling, too, because I am making such a big ass of myself. So he says, "I'm going to twist this tooth to see if there is any pain, and if there isn't we are going to pull that baby out." He twisted the tooth and there was pain, but he pulled it anyway! I had a nervous reaction in my leg, why there I do not know. I started kicking, and I kicked all of his equipment on the floor. All of his tools are all over the place. They were flying in every direction. I jumped out of that chair, leaping around the room, and she was laughing so hard she had to get out of there. He finally gets me settled down. We pick everything up. He said, "Take the salt water, do this and do that, and you'll be all right, kid. But as a favor to you, I think you better go out the back way." He didn't want me to have to go past her because I would be embarrassed, so he had me go out his back door. Now that's the story of my life. Every time I thought I was a big deal, God straightened me out in a hurry.

Jack Clifford Was God's Way of Being Nice to Western Michigan

STEVE RHODES

Steve Rhodes

Steve Rhodes is a former professor at Western Michigan University and former director of Western's School of Communication. Rhodes transformed the Communications Resource Center into the Clifford Center for Media Education and Outreach.

I met Jack when I was a rookie administrator at WMU. I had been a faculty member for twenty-five years at that point, had never planned on doing anything but being a full professor and teaching my classes. Somehow I got hoodwinked into taking over as the chair of the department. At that point, I knew very little about what that leadership role would involve, and all of a sudden I found myself being introduced to this wonderful gentleman I was supposed to wine and dine and talk fundraising with. I said to the president, "I know nothing about fundraising. Why would you stick a rookie in that kind of position?"

Well, Jack made it extremely easy because the first class I took him to was a leadership class. The students were absolutely enthralled with his life story. He ends the story and the class period with the statement, "Now I'm here because I've decided it's time to give back."

Well, when you're absolutely scared to death about fundraising and your first prospect leads off by opening the door that says, "I'm now here to give back"—wow! Jack made it extremely easy to then take on that role.

I took the lead along with Jack in terms of trying to establish how he wanted to give back to the university. We drafted a proposal that met all of his wishes. As can happen with a rookie, the next thing Jack and I know, I'm no longer involved. The development people and others have stepped in, taken my proposal, redrafted it, and essentially irritated Jack. He more or less said, "I'm out of here."

Fortunately, Jack and I had gotten off on such a good footing that, in spite of what development did, he and I got together again and essentially told the president, "Keep the development people out of here and away from Jack, and he and I will do this together." We then proceeded for the next couple of years to put together a wonderful proposal that allowed us to give Jack the kind of recognition we wanted to honor him with in the school of communications.

More significant was us saying, "Jack, we don't care about the money or a gift. What we want is for you to come back, be here, and continue to talk to these students and to mentor them." That's what he wanted as his primary focus, and in the long run, that became the center of his involvement. Anything he and I were able to do on the fundraising side became secondary. Without Jack's initial gift, we would not have been able to do any of what we did after that. As a result, we had a very successful initial fundraising campaign, and that legacy Jack started has continued.

The first thing he wanted to do was to go to the student radio station. The next thing I know, his jacket is off, the tie is loose, and he's sitting down with a bunch of eighteen-year-old kids who are playing contemporary music. They were just having a devil of a time together. I thought, *This is easy. All I've got to do is get Jack together with the right students, and everything else takes care of itself.*

He often came for Homecoming. One year, Jack worked his way up to the announcer's booth at Waldo Stadium. The folks doing the play-by-play had invited Jack to be on air with them. During halftime, he is entertaining all of Kalamazoo by talking about his first football broadcast, which took place from a dorm since he wasn't even at the game. He had a buddy who'd driven to the game who was communicating with him via phone, while he's making up the play-by-play. He was always comfortable, regardless of the situation and the circumstance.

The same kind of thing happened a few years later. We were getting together to do a fundraiser for the baseball field. There was a reunion of one of Western's greatest baseball teams. I had stopped over to the festivities with Jack. We were not really invited, but Jack wanted to stop because he remembered being the play-by-play announcer for the baseball team. We walk into the room, and I'm thinking, *Okay, this may not be a good idea. It's like crashing a wedding. I don't know any of these folks. I really don't know the development people, and I'm walking in with Jack.*

I just laid low, and, again, the next thing I know, I hear all this laughter, and three or four of these guys who remembered Jack doing the play-by-play have all gathered around one another, and, once again, Jack's into the play-by-play. Jack has so much charisma that he's going to charm his way into any situation, any circumstance.

One of those times both my wife and I fondly remember connects to where we are now with Jack and Bev. About a year after he lost Marguerite, he came back. When he didn't stay at our home, he would stay in Marshall, Michigan, which is nearby. He loved to go to Win Schuler's, a famous area restaurant in Marshall.

Well, the next thing we know, over dinner, he's telling us that he's dating, and he wants our advice. Eventually we went out to Scottsdale to meet Bev. What a delightful end of that story where he went from that period of obvious grief and mourning to sounding like a sixteen-year-old about dating a wonderful woman like Bev. That has been just a delightful relationship.

On his last trip to Kalamazoo, we had gone downtown. Jack was talking about where he once broadcasted from. He was pointing up at the top of a building. We're thinking that we'd love to get him up there so he could see it again, but it was not an exit point. It's simply a fire escape. But we Photoshopped the picture to put him on top of the building he used to broadcast from.

The weekend he got the WMU Distinguished Alumni Award was unforgettable. Jim Hickey of ABC News was there and stayed at the Kalamazoo Radisson, as did Jack and others. On the first night Kalamazoo had tornado activity, where it went beyond a warning. The Radisson evacuated all of the rooms, the bar, and the restaurant and herded everybody into the basement for the tornado warning. Well, apparently Jack Clifford and Jim Hickey of ABC News had a delightful time and proceeded to entertain this entire group of folks over stories. Picture all of these distinguished folks and alumni down there in the basement in their pajamas listening to Jack Clifford and Jim Hickey.

Jack had a co-honoree that evening, Roz Abrams, a prominent CBS anchor from New York. You would have thought Roz was a trained comedienne because she had the audience in stitches. Normally at these kinds of black-tie award dinners, you don't typically get speakers up there that can actually engage an audience and have them laughing.

Then Jack got up there and began to go through the routine of "How in the world do I ever follow what we just saw?" It was a little like Dean Martin and Jerry Lewis. Jack proceeded to give his speech by playing off of what Roz had said and done. It was that whole image of this highly distinguished gentleman following this dynamic woman at the podium, and Jack had everyone in stitches, too.

**President John Dunn, Western Michigan University,
at the Clifford Communications Center.**

Choice Voice

GARRARD MACLEOD

Jerry Macleod

Garrard Macleod retired in 1999 from a forty-year career at Western Michigan University's public radio station, WMUK FM. For thirty of those years, he was a professor and general manager of WMUK.

My history with Jack doesn't go quite back to when he was three years old or in the third grade or anything. I met him in an interpretive reading class at Western Michigan University, which was then Western Michigan College, it must have been about 1954, 1955, somewhere in there.

Zach York was the head of the speech department at the time. He taught interpretive reading, and Jack and I were in this rather large class held in a little theater on campus. I had read something, a poem or something. We all had to read something on the first day of class.

Anyway, Jack collared me out in the lobby of the theater after we got done with this class. He said, "So, you're Jerry Macleod. Well, my name is Jack Clifford, and I'm in the class there, and I heard you read." He said, "You seem to have a fairly decent voice, and I've just become the manager of WIDR, the student radio station. We're looking for somebody to read newscasts. We just got a United Press teletype through the sponsorship of Lucky Strikes cigarettes so we can now do newscasts. Would you be interested in auditioning for this job?"

I said, "Well, yeah, I suppose." I explained that I didn't know anything about WIDR. I lived in town. I didn't listen to the dormitory radio station. "But," I said, "does this pay something?" He said, "No, no, it's volunteer. Everybody's a volunteer, but you need to be there on a regular basis if you decide to do this." I said, "Well, that sounds sort of interesting. I'll come over." He said,

"Come over around four o'clock this afternoon, and I'll give you an audition," and he had to explain where it was. It was in a little shack that had been the chicken coop for the agricultural school. The university had bought the property.

Anyway, I showed up to this little shack at four o'clock that afternoon. He showed me the teletype, which I had never seen before, and he ripped a couple of pieces of paper off of it and kept pumping the paper out. He said, "Here, read this." I read it. I don't remember what it was, some bulletin or other. He said, "Okay, that was pretty good. Here, read this one." While I was in the middle of that, he said, "Here, a bulletin is just in. Read this." I had to switch gears and read. I did a bunch of his stuff for about ten minutes. He said, "Well, that was great. You're hired."

I said, "Okay, what do I do?" and he said, "Well, there's a newscast at five o'clock today. I'll engineer, and you do the newscast. Fifteen minutes; you've got about an hour to get this stuff ready. Just tear off these stories. There's a national news summary. You can read that." I thought it was a piece of cake until I got into the little studio, and there was a microphone there, and I realized that, all of a sudden, somebody was going to get me some kind of a cue, and I was going to have to read on demand, and that freaked me out. I mean, I got really nervous and began sweating.

Anyway, the cue came. I read the stuff, but I kept hyperventilating. I was gasping for breath, but I finally got through it. In the meantime, he was laughing in the control room at my discomfort. But we got through that, and he said, "It will get better. You'll get used to it."

I got involved with the student radio station, and Jack was the one who involved me, and that became my career, as it turned out, not at the student radio station of course but broadcasting. He was great. We formed a friendship.

He lived in a rooming house not far from where my parents lived. I was living at home because we lived close to campus, and there was no point in my living at the dormitory. I would go over to his place, and eventually we started writing scripts for these silly radio dramas we would do. He had a program on the station called "The Hate Hour." That was a late-night program. I can't remember whether it was every night or once a week, but it was this terrible hodgepodge of funny bits and news stories and music, and he would write these funny comedy sketches. I found the script to one not too many years ago, going through some junk I had saved from my days at school. It was a Sherlock Holmes take-off. Apparently I played Holmes and he played Watson, and it was full of atrocious puns and old gags. It was pretty funny, as I read it these many years later. It was an old carbon copy of a script, and Jack had either forgotten about it or misplaced his, and I made a copy of it and sent it to him several years ago. So we have a record of this fun piece from years ago.

Jack and I formed a pretty close friendship. He had a bunch of crazy guys that lived with him in this rooming house. We all became fairly close. Then he and his buddies would come over to my parents' house. I have three brothers, and we're all close in age. We would do stuff together at the house—drink beer, play poker. He and I continued to be on air at WIDR.

Jack and I and mutual buddies of ours would get together on weekends. We were all underage. Jack was twenty-one, maybe, but he wasn't twenty-one the first time we started going to this bar called Chuck and Millie's out on South Westnedge Street in what is now Portage. It wasn't called Portage then, but it was outside the city limits. We could get served underage there. We would order this concoction called a sloe gin fizz, an atrocious thing made with sloe gin, which is hard to find now, fizz water, and I don't remember what else. Lime juice, I think.

They had this funny-looking little guy who played an electric organ and a sleazy-looking little drummer. They would play music, and the people danced. We would go out and drink beer and sloe gin fizzes and harass the customers and then escape before we got thrown out.

Later Jack got a job at WKMI, which was a local five-kilowatt commercial station, and he worked there for quite a long time. He had a late-night disk jockey show there called *Cruising with Clifford*. It was very popular, and Jack has, of course, a hysterical sense of humor. I would go up and visit him at WKMI. I was still finishing up my degree and working at WIDR. I would go up and visit him at the station. He would put me on the air, and we'd clown around. He probably wasn't supposed to do that.

That's my basic early history with Jack. He's the one who got me started in radio. I later became the manager of the public radio station at the university and was there for forty years, from 1959 until 1999.

Incidentally, WIDR is still going. Jack was in at the very founding of that station in 1953. Now instead of an interdorm station, it's a low-power FM station. It pretty much covers Kalamazoo County and has a pretty good listening audience.

The upshot is I came along at the right time with regard to finding Jack Clifford, or him finding me, or us finding each other, and then sticking to that career like he stuck to his. He became wildly more successful than I did, but, in my own mind, I contributed, I think, to the culture and well-being of the Kalamazoo area through my association at the public radio station there. It has actually become a real force in the broadcasting industry around Kalamazoo.

I see Jack every spring in May. He gives his scholarship awards up at his school in Grand Rapids. Then he comes down to visit people at the university in Kalamazoo. He and I always have dinner. One time, we tried to get a sloe gin fizz at a fancy restaurant in the hotel where he stayed, and they had never even heard of sloe gin, so we were vastly disappointed.

He's a real success story. His parents were lovely people, but they didn't have a lot of money. Probably he wouldn't have gone to college except for the principal at his high school. He saw some talent in Jack and told him if he got his act together, got his grades up, he would see to it that he went to college. And he did. So that's why Jack has established this scholarship at Ottawa Hills High School in Grand Rapids. It's named in honor of the principal who helped Jack along the way.

He's given a lot of money to Western Michigan University as well because he figured that if it wasn't for them providing him an affordable education, he would never have been able to— well, that's not true. Jack would have been successful eventually somehow, but it made it easier for him, the education he got. He would have succeeded regardless because he has that drive, intelligence, and sense of humor, and he's a great people person.

Western Michigan Needs a Quarterback, a Halfback, and Jack Clifford Back

LEIGH ARDEN FORD

Leigh Arden Ford is a professor and director of the School of Communication at Western Michigan University and holds a doctorate in organizational communication from Purdue University. Dr. Ford's research interests emphasize supportive communication, the communication of health messages within disenfranchised communities, and contextualized understandings of health communication practices.

Leigh Arden Ford

I first met Jack in 2005. I was teaching a course in leadership, and he was on campus and had spent the day with our then-director Steve Rhodes and had met the president. He came back to our campus building, and I happened to be in the hall. Of course I was charmed by him.

I was getting ready to go off to my class, and he asked if he could come with me. He went to my leadership class and for about forty-five minutes talked to the students about his life story and his gratitude to Western but also about the significance of communication and the leadership role and how he really felt grateful that he had had the discipline of communication to call on as he moved through the business world and how important it was to his success.

The students were enthralled because everybody watches the Food Network, of course. They were pretty excited about that. But just having him share his story and being so open to them was really thrilling. So that's when I first met him, and we became friends, so to speak. When he would come back to campus, he remembered me well. Every time he would come for a campus visit, that was while Steve was director of the school, we'd spend a little time together and get caught up and that sort of thing. And then when I became director of the school, he was very supportive of me, and very supportive always financially of the school, but also just being our cheerleader and our champion, both on campus but also in the Arizona community.

On one of Jack's visits home, he was on his way from here to a wedding of a nephew or niece on the East Coast somewhere. Marguerite was not with him, and I drove him to the airport. As usual, he gave me a hug and said, "See you soon." I know this sounds crazy, but I just had a funny feeling, like something wasn't quite right. I remember actually saying that to someone when I went to work on Monday. He left on Saturday afternoon. When I went to work on Monday, I said, "I just had a funny feeling when I said goodbye to Jack."

That was the weekend Marguerite died. I don't know if I've ever even told Jack that. It was just a weird feeling. And actually the feeling was more about Jack, that something might happen to him as opposed to Marguerite. It was later that day or the next that we heard he had come home and found Marguerite dead. Of course, we were very sad for him because he talked so fondly of her. It was just kind of a weird coincidence, I guess you'd say.

Jack made a significant contribution to WMU. It's an endowment that supports our Clifford Media Center, which we're very grateful for. It helps us buy equipment for students and faculty and with outreach projects from the center. It helps maintain the center, period. It's become a community meeting place for our department.

This past year we had a big donor celebration to cap our ten years of campaigning to raise funds for the school. Jack was the prime contributor and one of the engines behind that campaign. It was a great celebration.

Jack's accomplished a lot, and he's a good soul. He cares a lot.

Chapter 3

By the Time I Got to Phoenix

Rich Wolfe

The Valley of the Sun, Except July When it's the Surface of the Sun

Phoenix was small, about 50,000 people. Maricopa County had about 100,000 people in the entire county. Today it's a hundred times larger, about 5 million people. I came to Phoenix at the right time. It was a relatively small town but ready to burst at its seams, and it went crazy. Slowly but surely towns such as Glendale, Mesa, Tempe, and Scottsdale became part of the Phoenix area. It went from the one hundredth market in television to the fiftieth, and by the time I left Phoenix, it was in the top ten. It was unbelievable growth, and I was lucky.

In the summer of 1957, I decided that I would take a well-earned vacation to Phoenix to visit my sister and parents who had recently moved west. My parents moved for their health and retirement and my sister and her husband Jim for a wonderful job opportunity. My sister was determined that I get a job in Phoenix. She was on a mission by the middle of the first of two weeks I had off. We went swimming a lot. They did not have a pool, but there were pools nearby. We did a lot of walking too. The air was so clear. I could sit on my sister's driveway and see for miles. That's how clear the air was. Simply beautiful. Anyway, we just talked, had a good time, and met some of her friends. She insisted I go look for a job in TV, although I still had the radio job in Kalamazoo and had not intended to stay. I was just there on vacation.

I borrowed her car and drove down to 16th Street, which looked like the main drag. I turned left, and there was Channel 3, KTVK. I went in, and a gal stopped me and said, "What can I do for you?" I said, "Well, I'm here visiting, and I have an appointment with your program director." She said, "You have an appointment?" I said, "Yes, my name is Jack, and I'm here for my appointment." Of course I didn't have an appointment, but a fellow by the name of

Don came out of his office. He was not much older than I—at the most, thirty years old. By now I was twenty-three. He said, "What can I do for you?" I said, "Well, I have an appointment with you." He said, "No, you don't." I said, "Yes, I do." He says, "Oh, all right. Maybe you do. I'm sorry if I goofed up." I said, "You're forgiven. I've never been in a TV station, so can I take a look?" He said, "We don't go on the air until noon." There was no *Today Show*, no *Tonight Show*; none of those existed in those days. In Phoenix, the networks were all spread out. They only produced live in New York, and they sent that signal out on coaxial cable to Chicago and then on to Phoenix.

Arizona didn't have the late or early programming. By the time the shows got to Phoenix, it was 4:00 or 5:00 in the afternoon instead of prime time. We had to create our own. Anyhow, I took a stroll with Don, and he said, "You know, it's kind of silly, but do you play football or baseball?" I said, "Yeah." He said, "How would you like to try out for our sportscaster job? We're going to do news for the first time." Many stations across the country, particularly the smaller markets, couldn't afford local news. He said, "Come back at 2:00 this afternoon and audition." I said, "Sure, thanks."

Then I went off to see the radio station, KTYL, which was on the Phoenix-Mesa Highway. There I met Jack Harris, the program director and general manager and a war amputee out of Fort Bragg. I explained who I was, and he said, "Do you want to take an audition?" I said, "Sure." He got a bunch of copy stuff, and I went into the booth for an audition. I did a reading for a radio show. He came out in the wheelchair, we went back to his office, and he said, "I'll hire you. You're pretty good." I said, "I love doing radio, I enjoy it, and I'll be living over in Scottsdale somewhere I hope." He looked me in the eye and said, "Son, television is the coming thing." I hadn't told him I had the audition later that afternoon. He said, "If you have a chance to get into TV, take it." Then I told him. He said, "I like you. You're a nice young man, and I'm going to give you some good advice. You go take that audition, and if they don't hire you, you got a job here."

At the TV audition I read the news and sports and did a stand-up commercial for a car dealer. They told me to come into the office, and I met with the program director, general manager, and the sales manager, Bill Ladow, who became the general manager as soon as I took the job. In any case, they said, "We've decided to hire you. Bill thinks as a commercial guy you have a strong personality and have a forceful attack on these commercials."

I called the radio station back in Kalamazoo and gave notice: "Hey guys, I'm going to go on TV in Phoenix, Arizona, and I'm coming back to get my car. How much time will it take you to find somebody?" They said, "Well, don't worry about it. Come on back. We'll work something out." So I went back, and the general manager said, "Phoenix is not going anywhere. It's way out in the hinterlands. It's dusty and dirty. You're making a *big* mistake."

I went back to Michigan and drove back to Arizona in my Ford Fairlane, a green and white two-door. I was twenty-three years old. One of my advertisers in Michigan gave me the car. I did a good job for him, so he got me a 100 percent loan. I had to put the cash out to buy the car over time. Like most cars then, it did not have air conditioning. I started driving around Phoenix and decided I had to do something. The heat was killing me. A place called Frigid King installed the air conditioning, but it put stress on the motor and almost ruined the car. But at least I could breathe.

My sister was thrilled out of her mind. She was hugging me—ecstatic. My dad, of all the things I had done to that point, was most impressed by seeing me on television. He thought it was a miracle. He couldn't get over it.

I joined Channel 3 on July 1, 1957. There was no video tape, and the only way we could prerecord was to use 16mm film. This was very costly, and we rarely prerecorded anything. All commercials and local programming were done live. The program following the news each evening was *Theater After Dark*, a feature-length movie. I both directed and did whatever commercials were required on camera. On one particular evening, Saggua Realty bought the sponsorship of the movie. A local on-air personality had been hired by the realty company to do their ads to promote Bonita Creek Ranch Estates. On rare occasion, that man failed to show up to do the commercials; therefore, I had to quickly put on a tie and sports coat and do the commercials in his place. This turned out, on one particular evening, to be a very funny incident.

On cue, I appeared on camera to state that the movie was sponsored by Saggua Realty, which was having the grand opening of their new development of summer cottages located in the cool country above the Mogollon Rim. But what I said was *Mongolian* Rim! The floor crew loved to see new announcers make mistakes; they were laughing. This distracted me further. I went on to say that this development was called "Bonita Cranch Reek Estates"! Every time I came to that line I repeated my mispronunciation. With this the crew laughed louder and harder. Eventually, I laughed as well. At the end of this episode, I thought I would surely be fired. This was a Friday night. The opening of the realty project was Saturday.

I arrived for work on Monday at 3 p.m. I saw a note in my mailbox from the general manager who wanted to see me ASAP. I went into his office, and he said to me, "I heard you had a real problem with the Saggua Realty commercials on Friday night. The advertiser called me at home late Friday and raised holy hell. He demanded I fire you and his company be reimbursed for the sponsorship of the movie." He then said, "Clifford, you are one lucky guy. The man called me back this morning and said, 'Did you get rid of that Clifford?' I said, 'No, I haven't talked to Clifford yet.' The advertiser then said, 'Great! We had our biggest weekend in history. I will gladly pay for the advertising if you keep that young man Clifford.'"

So, now, I'm really a stud. I'm young. I'm on TV. I had a car with air conditioning. It was July 1957. I was hired to do the Union Oil sports report on television. Union Oil operated in eleven western states and bought the local 6 p.m. sportscast on Friday nights.

The show originated from Los Angeles and was fed to the western states by microwave. The host was Elroy "Crazylegs" Hirsch, a great football player. The Reverend Bob Richards, an Olympic champion, was the first to do that show. They would do a half-hour show, with the first fifteen minutes from L.A. Then guys like me in regional markets would take over and do ten minutes. So, I did the Union Oil Sports Club for ten minutes for Phoenix, Albuquerque, Tucson, and Denver. We had a microwave system among all of us.

I was young and enthusiastic. I didn't want the ten minutes I had on this show to just be me sitting there talking about high school sports. In Phoenix the Olympic diving coach, Dick Smith, had a program for disabled and handicapped children. I invited Smith and his special program to be on my ten-minute show. I borrowed a portable pool. I had the local fire department fill it with 11,000 gallons of water. Friday night arrived, and I decided to do a dramatic entrance. All the children and I were in the swimming pool. We took the network cue, and I arose from the water like King Neptune on camera and they stupidly handed me a microphone. Lightning literally danced across the pool, knocking out all the kids, and I had the presence of mind to throw the microphone as far as I could. That, of course, ended the show and happily all the kids were OK and so was I.

In April 1958 there was a function called the Front Page Ball, which was part of the Press Club. It was made up of reporters and writers for magazines, newspapers, and so on. Our company was a member, but they never had anyone go to it. It was held at the Hotel Westward Ho, the big one downtown. The station wanted someone to represent them. I dressed well. I had good suits, so they suggested I go. I said, "I don't know anyone. I've only been here for a few weeks. I don't have a date." They said, "We'll get you a date." As luck would have it, the news director, Ray Thompson, had a next-door neighbor whose little girl was going into the third grade over at Madison School. Her teacher, Peggy, short for Marguerite, was my age. Ray asked if she would go with this guy at the TV station to the function for one night.

She said, "Absolutely *not*. I don't go on blind dates. I don't know what he looks like." Thompson said, "All you've got to do is turn on the TV station, and you can see him." "No, I won't do it," she replied. "I just don't do that. I go out with someone else." But then, Gil Wang, the principal at Peg's school, had been the college sweetheart of the lady next door with the child. He called Peggy into his office. "Listen, this is a nice guy. He's well thought of. He needs a date just one time, just to go to this thing he has to do," he said. "Well, have him call me," she said.

I called her. She sounded delightful and finally agreed to go. When I went to pick her up at 7 p.m. that Friday night, she wasn't ready. I stood outside. All I had was East Coast clothing. I'm sweating profusely and getting irate. She was holding me up, and I didn't think it was very nice. I said to myself that I'd give her ten more minutes, and then I'm leaving. She can go to hell. I'll go to the damn thing without a date. So, ten minutes goes by and she finally comes to the door. I had never seen a prettier, more delightful girl in my life. She was beautiful! Talk about hitting a home run, I hit a whole dozen!

People in the broadcasting business feel that broadcasting is the most important thing in the world. But a lot of other people don't. They think teaching and many other things are more important. This Peggy hears all of my blabber about how wonderful broadcasting is. I think to myself, *How can I impress her?* Here I am talking about broadcasting and she is trying not to look bored. I told her this is a ball, but I don't dance. I had only had a handful of dates all through college. I was working all the time! Girls were a great mystery to me.

In any case, we go to this ball, and everybody is having lots of fun. Finally, she says, "We can dance. Can't we try to dance?" So, we took two or three steps; then she said, "We had better sit down." So I fell in love. I pursued her. She thought I was attractive. When I took her home, I said, "Is there any way that I can see you again?" She said, "Oh, sure! I'm having a big party back at the apartment on Sunday. Why don't you come and be my date?" That was Friday night and then I'm with her on Sunday again!

We went out to dinner. I spent time at her apartment. She came down to the station to listen to me. I really fell for her and she for me. We didn't have any money so we would do things like drive up to Sedona to picnic in the woods up there. We would go down by the creek and neck. We were just kids. In July, on one of our visits to Sedona, we picnicked by Oak Creek. We stayed too long and the sun went down. We had to climb out of the creek area. I turned her around so that she was facing me, and I kissed her. I said, "You know, I think we should get married." She said, "I think we should, too." In October 1958 we were married, just six months after we met.

I promised her that when I married her I would learn to dance. You learn to dance just by dancing. After a while I could dance all right. After I retired, I went to Fred Astaire Studios for twelve years. In the first year, I fell in love with dancing. It's a lot of fun! If I had known at fifteen what I learned at forty-five, I would have quit football and danced. When God took that rib from Adam, it was the dancing rib. Women love to dance and men don't, for the most part. So, when men can dance, women love them—and guys hate them.

When relatives' children were married, I danced with every one of the bridesmaids. Everyone was crazy. They would line up for me. I rose all the way up to silver in the dancing contests. Over a period of ten years I danced in hundreds of contests all over the world. Even today, when I do my exercises in the pool, I like to dance.

My career improved rapidly after my marriage to Marguerite. She was working days, and I was working nights so I never saw her. So I asked for a job in sales, and for the first year, I still did the sports, but I also worked all day selling. And eventually, the selling became more productive. I dropped off the air to focus on selling to spend more time with my wife.

I had a wonderful life with Marguerite. We had two children, Jay and Kristin. Her death, from a heart condition, two days before our forty-ninth anniversary, was devastating. I don't know what happened. When I came home, she was dead, lying in the bathtub. Five hundred people came to her funeral, all of my broadcast friends and all of her friends. I was on the opera board and she was on the symphony board. We were really active in the community.

I have always been an energetic person, and when I get interested in something, I really go after it. I thought being a sportscaster on television was next to being in heaven. I loved sports. I got to meet a lot of nice, interesting people. Television was secondary to radio in those days. About 25 to 30 percent of homes had TV sets, but every home had a radio. We were limited. We had no equipment to go outside the studio and do a television program. The cameras were the size of a small car, so everything had to be brought to the studio. There was very little going on in Arizona in 1957, except that Arizona State College, now Arizona State University—the largest university in the nation—had one hell of a football team. They were ranked twelfth in the United States and won the WAC (Western Athletic Conference).

In August, even to this day, Arizona pretty much dries up and blows away for a while. People start coming back in October or November because it is so darn hot. It isn't like it used to be when the town closed up, but there's still not a lot going on. Keep in mind, in those days there were no West Coast Major League Baseball teams. Kansas City was as far west as they came. Finally the Dodgers and the Giants moved west. That helped because you had something in the same time zone to talk about. Later we had some boys from Arizona State really hit it big like Rick Monday and Reggie Jackson. This hadn't happened yet, so we had nothing to brag about.

I had to do something. I did all of the announcing and directed commercials and kid shows. I was on *Jungle Jack* once a week, but I never had time to really get prepared. I was rushing around directing shows, writing shows, doing shows, and at the same time collecting every bit of sports information I could by phone and telefax. I could not leave the building very often. I did not have TV equipment to go out with. If I did an interview, it had to be in the building. Most of these athletes weren't too excited about coming into the studio. I tore the stuff off the teletype each day.

A he-man by the name of Julio Hernandez in a pre-Olympic competition had set three world weightlifting records up in Prescott, Arizona. Prescott is cooler in the summertime and where Phoenix people retreat to get out of the heat. Hernandez made these wonderful new records, and I was excited. I finally found news that had something to do with Arizona, not just how hot it is on the ball diamond or what is happening in Little League.

One day, I'm in a room that had double-paned soundproof windows looking out into the studio. Ray Thompson, the news guy, sat at the far end next to the wall, which separated this whole thing from the control room. We could vaguely hear what was going on in the control room. We got used to it and actually didn't pay much attention to it. The cameramen were out in the studio shooting through those double-paned glass windows. I had multiple jobs, but Ray only had the one; all Ray had to do was news, and he did a great job of it. Ray took all sports news from the teletype and threw it in this big hopper. I would dash up there and go through this stuff to find something to report on. I would quietly slip in the small studio, sit down, adjust all of my little equipment, and get ready to go on the air. Ray would say, "Now with the Arizona sports round-up, here's KTVK's sport's director, Jack Clifford." I'd say, "Thank you, Ray." And that's when I turned to the microphone and said, "Wow, we've got big news here in

Arizona. A real he-man, Julio Hernandez, made a 160-pound snatch tonight." I said that! I realized that the word *snatch* had just come out of my mouth, and I had done a very bad thing. Ray was laughing so hard, he got on his knees, went under the desk, and stuffed a hankie in his mouth.

I'm sitting there gasping, and through an air vent I could hear Lloyd, our director, say, "Did he say *snatch*?" I could hear it through the walls. "Did Clifford, that son of a bitch, say *snatch*?" Oh God! I'm trying to control myself, but I'm laughing, too, because of the image I am projecting. Finally I had to get the word out that we were talking about weightlifting. I said, "And then he followed that with a big 385-pound clean-and-jerk." We all went into hysterics, and they faded to black and started the movie early. Somehow, there were no complaints.

I was also required to be Bob, the Carnival Pitchman, on *Comedy Caravan*. It was a live show in the studio with parents and kids and we gave away prizes. It was a fake circus. I was in this little booth, "Come one, come all . . ." I did the commercials blind. I never had a chance to rehearse them because I was doing all of this other stuff, that's the only excuse I can give. Invariably, there was some little gimmick the shop would send down that I could not make work. We had a toy helicopter that was supposed to fly up and then come down. One time, it flew into the audience and almost knocked the kids over. No matter what we did, we somehow screwed it up. The last night of the show, I had a hard time with the commercials again. We bid everybody farewell for the season, and then I go into my little booth and say, "This show has been brought to you by . . ."; I got through all of that. Then I was supposed to pull down the shade. The shade wouldn't come down. Finally I jerked it and the whole damn set came down! It was like dominos—boom, boom, boom, boom. People were screaming! Fortunately, they didn't blame me. They didn't even know what caused it. But that was the end of that show.

Ray Thompson, the news guy at Channel 3 back in the 50s, had become a personal friend, like an older brother. When Channel 3 stopped doing the news, he lost his job. He was offered the job of promotion manager at Channel 12, NBC. So he went over to Channel 12, which in that day did not do the news. Then he called to tell me about a sales job he thought I should apply for, and I got it.

I was hired at KTAR-TV Channel 12 in Phoenix as a sales guy in 1962. It was so professionally run that I was inspired and worked my ass off. I worked Saturdays and Sundays, whatever they wanted me to do, and became their top salesman. In 1968, they were owned by the John Louis family. They were the largest stockholders of Johnson's Wax. It was the largest privately held company in the world.

I really did well at Channel 12. I loved it and I was appreciated. In 1968 they made me the sales manager. On January 1, 1970, I became president. They called me upstairs to the owner's office. I thought I was going up just to get my Christmas bonus from Karl Eller, the big honcho at Combined Communications. Karl said, "We had a good year. How would you like to be president?" "Sure. Some day when I have the right . . . I'm ambitious. I want to get ahead." "You're not hearing me," responded Karl. "What do you mean?" I said. "Now—today! This minute." "Sure!" I thought he was kidding me. "You cannot tell anybody. You cannot tell your wife. Not until we come back." This is December 23rd. "When we come back after the New Year's holiday, we will announce to the entire staff that you are taking over." Ray Schmucker had been the president for the past several years but was retiring. "But you can't say anything." I was bursting inside, but I couldn't even tell Marguerite. I had no idea they were going to offer me that. I was happy being sales manager.

So, on January 3, 1970, when we all went back to work, we met in the big studio. I'm standing up there with Karl, and he says, "Jack is kind enough to accept the position as president and general manager of the company. Schmucker is retiring, and we thank him very much for his work." And that was it. It was sort of like being hired as the first baseman for the Yankees. Once you're in, you're in. You're never going to play minor league baseball again. So, I got in and did well at it. At the time I was only thirty-five years old!

From January 1970 until late summer of 1974, I managed Channel 12 NBC-TV in Phoenix and assisted in negotiating and acquiring ABC Channel 5 KOCO, in Oklahoma City. Combined Communications asked me to oversee both channels. The Oklahoma City negotiations were a wonderful experience for me. I truly became a businessman because of that. In 1974 parent company Combined Communications Corporation acquired the ownership of the ABC TV affiliate in Denver and the NBC affiliate for Little Rock, Arkansas. I was never notified or included in this deal. I was informed after the deal was made, and I was no longer in charge of the television group. I was going to inherit a new boss. Of course I was disappointed that I was left out of the negotiations and my responsibilities were curtailed. But I loved Channel 12 and loved being in Phoenix. Unfortunately, or maybe I should say *fortunately*, my new boss disliked me but had to put up with me because I had successfully managed a TV station for the company.

Within a year, I was asked to leave Phoenix and move to Atlanta to be president and general manager of Channel 11 ABC. Fortunately, my family supported me fully in this move. My son Jay was eleven and my daughter Kristin was nine. The station in Atlanta was in disrepair. It didn't compete very well technologically with the stations in the market. I was there only seventeen months, but during that time I took the station to profitability. I had a 2,000 foot tower installed for the transmitter and spent a great deal of time building the station's image. Throughout this entire period I was harassed by my new boss. He finally won and I left the company. One door closes and another one opens in life and this was the beginning of a blossoming career.

Age thirty-six, first day as president of KTAR (now KPNX) Channel 12, NBC TV, 1970.

They Didn't Know Much about Horses. They Knew They Had Four Legs and Gave Milk, That's about It

RAY ODOM

Ray Odom

Ray Odom, Mr. Country Music of Arizona, in radio and television. Former general manager of KJJJ Radio, for the past thirty years Odom has been a successful trainer of thoroughbred racing horses.

I've known Jack for years. I was doing a television show on Channel 3 in Phoenix many years ago. It was a Saturday country music live band show. We'd bring in big guest stars like Johnny Cash, Willie Nelson, and Marty Robbins.

I got to know Jack really well. He has some very funny stories. You probably are familiar with that story about the senator who had a makeshift boom microphone fall and hit him on the head and knock him out. He has so many other great stories.

Jack has just been one of the greatest guys. I've trained horses for him and his lovely wife. Jack spent a considerable amount of money buying horses. They had one horse, an A. P. Indy colt. It was one of the great stallions of the world, and his stud fee was $450,000. They bought this A. P. Indy colt for $650,000 as part of a syndicate. They didn't own this one singularly.

One day the owners called me and said, "Ray, that horse is just not doing well. He didn't do well in Florida, Kentucky, or New York."

Jack said, "I have the first right of refusal to buy him for $25,000. Do you think he would do well at Turf Paradise in Phoenix?"

I said, "Well, why don't you call the horse's trainer, Bill Mott. He's a very honest man. Ask him if the horse is sound. If he is sound enough to run, he's certainly worth any $25,000." He called me right back and said, "The money has already been wired."

I had the pleasure of training that great horse. Jack came out with his camera and made the DVD for us. We had a lot of success with that particular horse. As a matter of fact, his beautiful wife Marguerite even went to the University of Kentucky for a while to learn about breeding. She went back to college. That's how much she was interested in the horse racing industry.

Marguerite and me at the Ascot Racecourse outside of London, 2005.

Wherever Jack went, he was hugely successful. As you know, he's got the greatest personality, and he's always got that great smile. People just love him. All the advertising agency people in Phoenix commented about what a wonderful person he is.

He started the Food Network, as you well know, and I believe he sold that for $150 million. He was just a genius in his field, and he said, "I sold it too doggone soon because it's worth a billion and a half now." But he said, "I didn't do too badly I took that $150 million and bought some TV stations up in Washington state." And he had tons of stock. We never did get into any figures about how much was involved, but it's none of my business. But he's just been an outstanding businessman.

He's a great speaker too. He's in the Arizona Broadcasters Hall of Fame.

Our apartment in London when we ran racehorses at Ascot, 2001-2005. Bonnie and Rollin Baugh, my horse racing manager, with Marguerite and myself.

Ascot Racecourse with Rollin Baugh (in gray top hat), my horse manager, 2006.

The Write Guy

CHRIS CALLAHAN

Chris Callahan

Chris Callahan is the founding dean of the Walter Cronkite School of Journalism and Mass communication at Arizona State University, vice provost of the Downtown Phoenix Campus, and CEO of Arizona PBS.

I first met Jack when we moved to the Valley in '05 to run the Cronkite School. It doesn't take very long to be in town with Jack Clifford, if you have anything to do with the media, before he comes across your radar screen. He was introduced to me by a colleague. He's one of those folks who has such a magnetic, charismatic personality that I felt like we were fast friends after about a twenty-minute meeting—just a wonderful guy.

Essentially I reached out to Jack and said, "Hey, you're one of the most important media leaders and media visionaries of the twentieth century. I'm trying to build a journalism school for the future. I need you. I need your thoughts. I need your ideas. I need you to be part of this team," and Jack was all in.

We would talk regularly about what we were trying to do here at the Cronkite School to create a highly professional, digitally focused journalism program looking ahead to not what the media is today but what it's going to be tomorrow and down the road.

Jack was so passionate about it; he said, "I want to be a part of this." He gave us a significant donation to name one of the spaces in the building, which proudly bears the name of Jack and his beautiful late wife, Marguerite.

Jack serves on our Cronkite endowment board of trustees. He remains an important advisor to me. I'm lucky just being able to tap into somebody like Jack, who is very generous with his time. He's been a mentor to me. He's been a mentor to our students, just a very important person here in our Cronkite school ecosystem. Of course, Jack developed a very close personal relationship with Walter Cronkite. It was really very touching. In fact, we flew to New York together when Walter passed away. The funeral was at St. Patrick's Cathedral, a closed event.

As smart as he is and as much of a visionary, that's how sweet of a guy Jack is. He's just the kind of person who will do anything for you. I feel quite lucky to call him a friend.

WALTER CRONKITE
51 West 52 Street
Suite 1934
New York, New York 10019

Phone: (212) 975-3627   Fax: (212) 975-1509

November 4, 2005

Mr. Jack Clifford
6221 E. Vista Drive
Scottsdale, AZ 85253

Dear Jack:

    With a dinner table as large as ours the other night, there is a certain sense of lottery in the companion we find at our elbow. Of course, with as distinguished a guest list as ours, the chance of drawing a winning ticket is considerably enhanced.

    However, I felt I won the grand prize as our conversation proceeded and the dialogue established such common interests in world affairs, our national problems and, most particularly, our concerns and proposed solutions for the bright future of our ASU Journalism School.

    I hope that we can get together when next you visit New York. I look forward to that meeting and should it not be sooner I shall eagerly await our next session in Phoenix.

    Meanwhile I shall look forward to your classical music channel.

All the best to you and Marguerite,

Walter Cronkite

The letter that began my friendship with Walter Cronkite in 2005.

The Boast of the Town

BILL MILLER

Bill Miller

Bill Miller is a founding member of Magic Dust TV. He is the producer of Right This Minute, *a viral national video show, and the former president and general manager of KTVK in Phoenix.*

My Jack Clifford stories are all about what a great guy he is and how helpful he is, especially as we were starting our latest syndicated show. He put us together with other people in the industry. He was just outstanding at that. He was a real cheerleader for us on the business side, and, as a friend, I don't know if you could ask for anybody who was nicer, more considerate, and more caring than Jack.

Jack and I also knew each other as he was involved with St. Joseph's Hospital in Phoenix. I was on the board there and was chairman at one time. Jack put a lot of his time and energy and, frankly, money into doing what he could to help St. Joseph's and Barrow's help people. For BNI, the Barrow Neurological Institute, he was really helpful and just a good guy, a good community person.

When We Were Young and Our World Was New

PHEBE THOMPSON

Phebe Thompson

Phebe Thompson was the first female radio announcer on WBZ Radio in Boston. She went on to sing pop music on the station and sang coloratura opera at the Royal Albert Hall in London. She was a commercial writer in Kalamazoo, Michigan, and Rochester, New York, and was the PR director for Arizona Health Plan, now Cigna.

My husband, Ray, had been one of the first to ever be on television. He was an anchorman and a news director. We decided that we did not want to stay in the cold Midwest anymore, so in 1957, we came down to Phoenix. There was no news on any station. My husband decided he would be the first news director and anchor at a Phoenix station, Channel 3. Jack came in about the same time.

Anyway, Ray and Jack were the originators of that newscast, and Jack was a very funny fellow. He's one of the funniest men I've ever met. He was always joking. He and my husband had a good time with early Arizona TV. Jack has a very good sense of humor, and he has a lot of good stories to tell about the early days in Arizona.

Just before the first broadcast, they had a segment with a company that had a little zoo with snakes. The snakes got loose. They couldn't find them all. My husband was terrified of snakes, and they didn't know where they were. That was a hard start. I don't think they ever found the snakes.

I introduced Jack to his first wife, Marguerite. She was called Peggy in those days. We were going to what they called a Front Page

Ball. It was one of the first balls ever connected with television. Jack was single and maybe twenty-four at the time. He didn't have a date. My next-door neighbor's third-grade teacher was Peggy.

Anyway, he came to the house with Marguerite before the Front Page Ball. My son was two years old. When he opened the door, he said, "Wow, what a smasher!" He thought she was so beautiful. They never forgot that. They always remembered my two-year-old saying, "Oh, what a smasher." I have no idea where he got that from.

Then, in fourteen months or so, Ray got a job starting the news on the NBC station. Jack said to him, "Well, if you ever find any jobs over there, call me." Some months later, there was an opening in the sales department. Ray called Jack, and Jack got that job. Jack was excellent at selling and became sales manager in a short time.

Then Marguerite and Jack were married. They couldn't have any children, so they ended up adopting. I said, "Well, you know, we got you a wife, and we got you a job. We're not going to do anything about those kids."

I didn't think Jack and Marguerite were going to hit it off that well. I thought it was just a one-night date. It really worked out beautifully. They were very happily married. It was very sad at the end.

But we were all raising families in the meantime and doing our thing. He was in Boston and in New England, and his career took off. He just did so beautifully and then was connected with the Food Network. He did very well. He was a boy that made good.

He always called my husband his big brother. They really had a very great bond together. They really loved each other. They were very different, but they really connected. I don't know why they connected so well. Their personalities were very different, but Jack had a lot of admiration for my husband. My husband knew his news, and he was a good journalist. Ray was a quiet man, dignified and quiet, but he loved Jack. They had such a good time together. They both laughed at each other. They were just very compatible, but you wouldn't think they would be.

The last thing we did with Jack was the Walter Cronkite dinner. They had a real Arizona Indian who got up and did that Indian music that goes on and on. Everybody was so tired of it. It went on for I don't know how long. Everybody was suffering listening to it. Then Ray just looked at Jack and said, "Just think. That was the last thing Custer heard," and that cracked Jack up. He laughed so hard. Then the whole table laughed, and pretty soon the guy stopped playing.

It Was a Ball

BOB ALLINGHAM

Bob Allingham

Bob Allingham was a well-known TV producer and director for Channel 12 (NBC) in the Phoenix market in the 50s and 60s.

Jack was a salesman of TV advertising time at a station in Phoenix when I worked at a competing station. I was known as the best commercial director in town. He had me produce some of his clients' ads because he knew I could make them far better than his production people could. He wanted experience and thought I was the guy who could do it, whether it was business for another station or not.

Jack didn't care what his station thought. He just wanted his clients served properly, and he thought I could do a better job. I was a director at that time, and he was a salesman. I don't think either station knew what was going on. That was probably our first business association. He knew I was good because we were a small market, and people know who's doing what and why.

Later, Jack came over and worked for our station, KTAR, as a salesman. He eventually became head of the whole operation.

He found out I played golf. For the opening of Sun City, Del Webb had a big tournament with media. Jack and I were partners and won it. So, from then on, every time there was a tournament for media or for whatever, he would call me, and we'd go out. That was interesting. I'd always been a good golfer.

Rich Wolfe

Picture Gallery

Age two and a half, Gary, Indiana, 1935.

**Howard Cosell at the grand opening of WXIA (ABC),
Atlanta, Georgia, August 1974.**

**Chris Schenkel, longtime ABC sports announcer,
with me and my son Jack Jay, 1974.**

Mary Morrison was major media buyer for the largest ad agency in Phoenix—Jennings and Thompson. She later went on to create her own ad agency named M Media. She is the founder and director of the House of Broadcasting. Mary sits on the endowment board of the Walter Cronkite School at ASU.

Jack and Beverly Clifford at the 11th Annual House of Broadcasting Gala.

Fundraiser for the AZ Opera sponsored by Gary and Jeanne
Herberger to cook my "world famous" chili at their house.
Left to right: Gary Herberger, Marguerite, Jeanne Herberger,
Ruth and Hugh Downs, 2000.

House of Broadcasting, Phoenix, Celebrity Salute
with Debbie Gaby, 2008.

My chili story in Chile Pepper magazine, 1997.

**My sister Rosejean's eighty-seventh birthday,
a week after my seventy-sixth, 2009.**

**My wife of nearly forty-nine years, Marguerite,
at a dance contest shortly before she passed away in 2007.**

**Beverly and me on a fishing trip to Nootka Lodge,
Vancouver Island, Canada, 2009.**

Presented by my class of 1951 with a painting that hung in my principal's office at Ottawa Hills High School, 2011.

Tom Chauncey, attorney representing Arizona Broacasting Association, Mary Morrison, long time friend and colleague in the ad sales business. Owner of M Media, with her sister, 2014.

**Eddie Fritz, longtime chairman of the
National Association of Broadcasters, May 1994.**

year, in an effort to give viewers more insight into their communities than local TV stations provide.

Colony's Portuguese Channel, which is produced at its Whaling City Cable TV headquarters in New Bedford, Mass., is distributed to systems in 36 New England cities with large Portuguese constituencies. And in Coral Gables, Fla., the Spanish-language Miavision channel caters to the local Latin American population with a programming paella heavy on local information and news.

In the latest ACE awards competition, Miavision's half-hour weeknight newscast, *Noticiero Miavision*, walked past four English-language nominees to win in the series news category. (Two of the other four finalists were from Colony systems, its U.S. Cablevision system in New York state and Lowell Cable Television in Massachusetts.)

Joe Langhan, Colony's director of programming, recalls that The Portuguese Channel was launched in 1976 as a

Colony's president, Bruce Clark (left), and its chairman, Jack Clifford, in Providence.

part-time network in an effort to increase the New Bedford systems' penetration in an area where about 60 percent of the population is of Portuguese descent.

But Clifford adds that Colony's local programming efforts also evolved out of a desire to make the cable systems a positive force within their communities. And doing the channels right required considerable effort.

"Most of the programming we had to produce ourselves," says Langhan. "We basically did anything. We did music videos before we even knew what music videos were. We started filming [the Portuguese community's] favorite singers back in Portugal, lip synching their songs in the park or on the beach."

The value of the channel became evident about two years after its launch, when the system bumped it up to a higher priced tier and transformed it into a full-time service. Within a month, about 20 percent of the system's 15,000 subscribers had called a special number to talk with Portuguese-speaking operators about signing up for the higher tier, according to Langhan.

The channel, begun as a co-venture with the local *Portuguese Times* newspaper, is still produced at Colony's New Bedford system. However, it is now wholly owned by the *Times*.

While Langhan scoured Portugal looking for product for the channel, a different kind of hustling has taken place at *Newscenter 13*, a program put out by Colony's systems in Fall River and New Bedford, Mass. Each of the show's three reporter/anchors covers three to five stories daily. A local district attorney drops in after work to deliver the sports. And when the men in the group get ready

CHANNELS / NOVEMBER 1989   43

**With president Bruce Clark when Colony was named
Cable Company of the Year, 1989.**

At the Challenger Center, Peoria, Arizona, with astronaut William Gregory, Space Shuttle Endeavour, 1995.

My exhibit at The House of Broadcasting. Scottsdale, AZ, 2014.

Named Executive of the Year in Cable Television, 1984.

Summer of 1974. Brand new president of ABC WXIA, channel 11 in Atlanta, GA at 38 years of age.

Myself with Bob Costas, Beverly and Phebe Thompson at the 29 Annual Walter Cronkite Award for Excellence in Journalism luncheon, 2012.

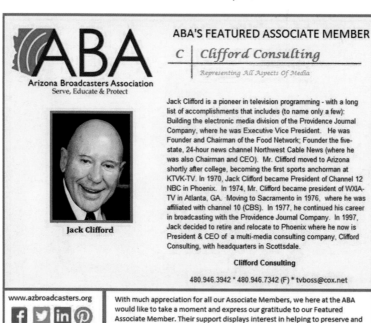

ABA'S FEATURED ASSOCIATE MEMBER

C | *Clifford Consulting*

Representing All Aspects Of Media

Arizona Broadcasters Association
Serve, Educate & Protect

Jack Clifford

Jack Clifford is a pioneer in television programming - with a long list of accomplishments that includes (to name only a few): Building the electronic media division of the Providence Journal Company, where he was Executive Vice President. He was Founder and Chairman of the Food Network; Founder the five-state, 24-hour news channel Northwest Cable News (where he was also Chairman and CEO). Mr. Clifford moved to Arizona shortly after college, becoming the first sports anchorman at KTVK-TV. In 1970, Jack Clifford became President of Channel 12 NBC in Phoenix. In 1974, Mr. Clifford became president of WXIA-TV in Atlanta, GA. Moving to Sacramento in 1976, where he was affiliated with channel 10 (CBS). In 1977, he continued his career in broadcasting with the Providence Journal Company. In 1997, Jack decided to retire and relocate to Phoenix where he now is President & CEO of a multi-media consulting company, Clifford Consulting, with headquarters in Scottsdale.

Clifford Consulting

480.946.3942 * 480.946.7342 (F) * tvboss@cox.net

www.azbroadcasters.org

426 N. 44th Street, Suite 310
Phoenix, Az., 85008
602.252.4833

With much appreciation for all our Associate Members, we here at the ABA would like to take a moment and express our gratitude to our Featured Associate Member. Their support displays interest in helping to preserve and protect free-over-the-air broadcasting. Thanks so much!

**Arizona Broadcasters Association's
Feature Associate Member.**

With Al McCoy, voice of the Phoenix Suns, and Ray Odom, Mr. Country Music in radio and television with Ray's wife Dolly, 2014.

My high school principal and mentor, Elmo Wierenga.

Jack Clifford confers with noted Western Michigan alum,John Hrycko of Dowagiac,at the annual Western Insider event at The Clifford Center in May of 2015.

**Joining the Providence Journal Company
in Rhode Island, 1977.**

Chapter 4

Providence was Divine
The Birth of the
Food Network

**Food Network booth at a cable convention
in Los Angeles, mid-'90s.**

I worked for the Providence Journal Company in Rhode Island from 1977 to 1997. The newspaper itself was a Pulitzer Prize winner and very well thought of within the business. It is the oldest daily published newspaper in the United States. However, it was weak electronically. I had run television and radio stations and was still a young man, in my early forties. They had heard about me and eventually recruited me.

The first thing I did was plan how we were going to expand the company electronically. Today, newspapers are waning badly and many have gone out of business, while broadcast is expanding. Now people are turning to cable and satellite for news, not the newspaper. People then were still reading the newspaper, but not the way they did, so they wanted a guy like me who had a background in these various businesses to join their company. They offered me a very good deal with stock interest. The only way you can ever make big money when working for somebody else is if you get stock in the deal.

I worked my way up from head of that division to become the number two executive in the company—executive senior vice president. I wanted very badly to develop program content. My background had been in program content, not technology. I didn't care how the product got there, just as long as it got there. I had a fair knowledge of television, radio, and cable. I understood technology, but it wasn't important to me. What was important was what we sent out. People did not buy cable TV, a radio, or a TV set just to look at it. They wanted something on it, and if you did not have something entertaining or exciting, they would throw it out. I felt we were missing the boat and that we didn't have good content on our various platforms.

The ProJo, as the Providence Journal Company is often called, had a small cable company that had limited service in parts of New England and upper New York state. They had 30,000 subscribers scattered around these small cable systems in rural areas. This was before cable multichannel platforms went into major markets, but ProJo was on the edge of doing that. However, a lot of laws and regulations prohibited that from happening because the FCC did not want duplication. Cable could bring more programming of increased variety. If you could prove to them that you were going to do something unique compared to what NBC, ABC, and CBS were doing, and do it better, they were happy with you. Slowly, I saw when I was being recruited by Providence that this cable thing might be pretty exciting.

I had always been a programmer. I had developed and directed newscasts, wrote scripts, and performed. I did all those things on the production side and became a salesman of some note. I sold advertising time on radio and television, but that, too, required production. You had to produce an ad, and I knew how to do that. Most of the people in radio and television did not. They were salespeople, not production people. I came up from the bottom. I didn't realize at the time it was a great advantage. I could sit down with businessmen and tell them what kind of ad should be run, how much it was going to cost to make that ad, and who they might hire, like a local celebrity. That would rub off on their product if it was a good product. I knew how to do all that, and I was good at it. I could even do the commercials myself. I thought I was a good announcer, and seemingly, other people did too.

I arrived at the Journal shortly before the FCC opened up cable TV to major markets. The company took advantage of this opportunity. We had cable systems in California, New York state, and Pennsylvania. We went from 30,000 cable subscribers to almost a million and were one of the top thirty cable companies in the country. I was chairman and CEO of Colony Communications, a wholly owned subsidiary of the Providence Journal Company.

Everything seemed to dovetail. I thought it was exciting. I liked production. I liked programming. I knew how to do it, so I started looking around for ideas. ESPN, which at that time was owned by Getty Oil, wanted me to become their president. Chet Simmons, who had been the head of NBC Sports, was then running ESPN. They didn't know exactly what they had. ESPN stood for Entertainment and Sports Programming Network, because they were going to do movies and other things, but sports were going to be the key part of it. It was not going to be an all-sports network at first because the over-the-air networks had game rights tied up. ESPN didn't know how much they could get. Well, we now know they got everything eventually. In any case, they needed somebody who knew how to sell advertising, who understood the marketing side of the business but who also knew production and presentation. I was recommended by McKinsey and Company to them as the potential president. Over the years I had gotten to know Chet Simmons from various TV conventions.

I had become the so-called guru in the industry for selling advertising locally, not necessarily nationally. What I mean by local is that my cable systems all sold local advertising time in those towns because we had available spots on all these networks, ESPN, CNN, etc. There were 360,000 opportunities to run ads on a cable company as big as ours. And I thought, *That's crazy. Why just throw those away? Let's take them and do them.* We did and started a little production unit in all of our cable systems around the United States.

We did a newscast serving some of these markets, for example, Fall River and New Bedford, Massachusetts. There were a lot of new things happening in that area of the country. That paid off handsomely because first of all, we had local advertising available, which I knew how to do, and second, it made a terrific public relations step toward the community that became dependent on us. Every fifteen years the city's cable franchising rights were up for renewal. I wanted city officials to think we were the greatest people on earth. Wouldn't you? They were the ones who had the keys to the kingdom, and without them and their support, they would get somebody else to run the cable business in their town. Should we lose the franchise, we would lose everything in that market.

All of a sudden, cable began offering some exclusive programming—networks like ESPN, CNN, and HBO. People wanted to buy HBO, not cable TV. How do I get this or that? How do I get CNN? They didn't care how it got there. All they wanted was the programming. Ted Turner has never owned a cable system and doesn't to this day, but he was making more money out of cable TV than any cable operator had ever come close to because he was getting paid every month at fifteen cents per subscriber. Once it was up on that transponder, he had no distribution costs. He was home free. It was like rain coming down. It cost to set it up, but once it is up, it is coming down and the cable operators paid for it and loved it. It gave cable a unique status in the community. People could only get CNN on their cable system. They could only see ESPN, HBO, Showtime, the Movie Channel, or the teenage stuff like music channels on cable TV.

MTV was another that I signed up right away because it was another market we were missing. We were broadcasting cable to a middle-aged crowd. But there were a lot of young couples that were getting married and liked younger music so I wanted to carry MTV.

Helen Copley, chairwoman of Copley Press, San Diego, mid-'80s.

We went from community to community obtaining requests for proposals to build cable TV systems. Most were in Florida and California. My idea was that we should obtain cable franchise opportunities in heavily populated regions of the United States. As luck would have it, the company had acquired a franchise in Hialeah, Florida, and had done nothing with it. We immediately set out to build the system there. We sought other franchises in the general region. We joined forces with a major newspaper operator in southern California, Copley Press. We began competing for cable franchises in Orange County and Los Angeles itself. We were successful. This was the basis for our rapid growth from 30,000 to nearly a million subscribers in the next few years. We eventually bought out Copley.

Some of the more offbeat things we did included competing in the regional chili contests in such places as Cypress, California. In my years in Arizona, I became a great fan of chili and made my own special brand. Cypress had a big annual chili cook-off. In the application we made to obtain their cable franchise, I mentioned that I would participate each year in their annual chili cook-off. They gave Colony the franchise and called my bluff, so I entered the cook-off for the next ten years. Finally, the tenth year, I won the darn contest, which was the regional chili cook-off of the International Chili Society.

Once, I was asked by the staff back in Providence to make my chili for a party. A young man who was in our development department loved it, but shortly after the party ended, his face became red and his breath became shortened. We rushed him to the hospital and discovered that he was allergic to cumin. He survived but never ate my chili again.

April 1985. Grand Opening of Copley/Colony Cablevision, Costa Mesa, CA. From left, Steve Hamblett, V.P. Pro Jo, Michael Isaacs, Director of Cable Franchising and Legal Services, Fourth from left, John C.A. Watkins, Chairman Pro Jo Company, sixth from left, me, to the right of me, Michael Metcalf, President of Pro Jo, 7th from right, Mel White, Director of Public Relations, Pro Jo.

The Providence Journal Company chose to go public in 1995. It had been a privately held company since 1828. The only way they were ever really going to capitalize was to go public. We convinced them to go public so we had to buy all these other partners out. Scripps-Howard is the one that finally bought the Food Network from us. In any case, they were one of our original investors. They had 200,000 cable subscribers, but we had to buy them out. We had a fair appraisal made and paid everybody off. Our partner in this whole thing was a company called Kelso Investments. They're on Park Avenue, right near where the Waldorf is, and a great bunch of guys. We were making a pitch, going around New York and other places in the country, talking with investment bankers to help finance our company.

The first place we called on was in Dallas, Texas, a company called T. Rowe Price. We were waiting in the reception area when this young man came out and shook hands. He said, "Who's the guy who started the Food Network?" I said, "Well, that's me." He said, "My wife told me if you can ever invest in that Food Network, get in there, baby. You don't have to make up bids. We're good to go."

We thought he was kidding. But we made our pitch anyway. Merrill Lynch was one of the underwriters. Bank of Boston, people like that. I flew around the world. I did the whole pitch in the European market. It was a fascinating time.

The Food Network is not big overseas, but the investment is. We went to bankers and investors in Britain, France, and Germany and made a pitch for them to help. We needed to get enough people involved in vetting the stock price that the underwriters guaranteed at the opening. When this finally happens, we don't own the stock anymore, the underwriters do. The only way they're going to do it is if they think the stock is going to rise.

The very first day the stock went from the opening price of around $15 to $22. I clanged the bell at the NYSE that day. The stock price stayed at $22 for quite some time, and then it went up even more. Of course, that gave us the money to do all these other things we wanted to do.

It sounds like I did it all, but I didn't. I was instrumental because it was my idea and I kept pushing for it, but right in the middle of all this we hired a new president. The president who hired me, Mike Metcalf, was my age. He was killed in a terrible accident. For two or three years after that, Steve Hamblett, the marketing director and vice president, ran the company. I had a great relationship with both Mike Metcalf and then after that Steve Hamblett. They believed in and supported me, but they needed a president.

They were able to hire Trygve Myhren. Trygve was the longtime marketing director for Time Warner Cable. Eventually he became president of that division. I knew Trygve from the cable industry and liked him a lot. I got called in on Thanksgiving one particular year when we were right in the midst of trying to put together the Food Network. They said they were hiring a president and I would have a new boss. That's not always the most comfortable thing in the world. I have been down that road a couple of times. When they said it was Trygve I was excited because Trygve and I were friends, and Trygve was quite well liked in the establishment.

A week later, I went out to California in the desert for a quarterly meeting of the NCTA (National Cable and Telecommunications Association) Board of Directors, and Trygve was there. We embraced and laughed about this whole thing. My partnership with Trygve was one of the most pleasant experiences I've ever had. In no way did that man do anything but help me, and I mean he appreciated me. He did not want to lose me. He was just terrific. He did more for me than anybody I've ever known in business, and he was smart.

I talk to him every once in a while, even now that we're all retired. Without Trygve, we would not have a Food Network. You've got to remember these were old New England guys sitting on this board of directors while I'm talking about spending millions of dollars. They were conservative, and that's why we eventually wanted to go public. We had to get away from them and do other things. Also, they finally figured out how much value the area I was responsible for had. The only way they could get the value out of it was to go along. They could not just go sell stock. Who were you going to sell it to? Another member of the family, a junior executive, buys it from Dad and Dad buys it back, so they needed to have a bigger market. That's why they eventually had to go public.

Mike Metcalf is the one who originally came after me. I turned the job down five times because I thought they were ultraconservative, and they were. But somehow or another, I managed to push it through, and with Mike's assistance, we worked it out. Unfortunately, Mike was killed, they think to this day by the Mafia. The Mafia is big in Rhode Island. Oh, none of this has ever been proven, but that's at least the rumor. Mike Metcalf was a sweet man, a good man. He would swallow hard at my ideas, but then he'd go ahead and do them.

I knew I'd gone with the right company when I went out and toured all the small cable companies, most of them in New York state, and I looked at the two radio properties in Providence. The radio in Providence was not so good. Anyway, I came back in with a proposal with how to expand their electronics side of the business, and it was pretty heady. We were talking about a lot of money. Metcalf sort of gulped, and I said, "Well, that's what you asked me to do." I said, "Well, now I'm going to quit. That's not what you promised me. If you're not going to help me out with this thing then I can go someplace else. All I need is money to take my family back to California. They are still there, and we'll just call this whole thing off."

That set him back in his chair, and he said, "I don't want to do that." I said, "Okay, are we going to do this or aren't we?" He said, "All right, do it." But he said, "One thing I want to tell you, you can never hurt one of our employees." That made such an impression on me. What a great guy! He was more concerned about his employees than with his own stock portfolio. Now, how many bosses have you ever met like that? I thought, *What an honor to work with this man; as long as he wants me, he's got me.* I almost wept in his arms. I had worked for so many jerks. I thought I'd died and gone to heaven.

A young man named Joe Langhan was working at our cable system in Fall River and New Bedford, very close to Providence. The Twin Cities are small. He was the program guy; whatever programming was done locally, he did. I was one of the few broadcasters that actually went over to cable. I had produced a lot of television programs, local stuff—news, weather, sports, musical presentations, and so on. Not only did I produce it, I announced it and everything else. I thought if we have these small markets, we should do news there. The reason I came to that conclusion was that I toured all of our existing operations at the Providence Journal Company. They had a cable business in Beacon, New York, some in Massachusetts, and one in Pittsburgh. These were small operations that had the capacity to do news if they wanted to. I wanted the place that would first do it to be near where I worked so I could go to see it, understand it, see how they did it. I knew how to produce a newscast.

When we contracted the cities to get the cable in there, we would have to guarantee a local channel. The best public relations I ever did in cable was to let them have a local news channel. It was their channel, but we did news on the same channel, and we owned the news part. We interviewed the mayor every week, or the governor, or an outstanding high school student, that sort of thing. It sounds silly, but it gave us tremendous public relations. You've got to have that in case things go haywire. Cable goes out, but not very often. Ours were very good cable systems, and we had a good technical staff. This built a good relationship with the initial franchise we were granted.

The initial franchise was for fifteen years, which enabled the cable company to amortize the cost of building the system before the contract expired. Every renewal after that was for ten years, so unless you're really screwed up, you're pretty much assured you are going to have a twenty-five-year life. By that time you have amortized the cost of building the cable system. Cable started out as a twelve-channel service, then Sylvania, RCA, and other electronic firms were able to up the number of channels you could carry through technical improvements from twenty to thirty-five, from thirty-five to fifty, from fifty and on. Every time that happened, you had to reassess the technicalities of the cable system, transformers, and new equipment so you could pass that many channels through it. Every mile or so, you had to put a new amplifier in, and those cost a lot of money. Also, the subscribers had to get new boxes because their box would only clear so many channels.

Joe Langhan was working in local programming in New Bedford. He was a bright hard worker but very shy. But he had good ideas, good concepts of video. I liked Joe and was very eager to do local programming. I saw the public relations as a benefit for our company. Plus I thought we could sell the ads in New York. The reason I found we could sell it is we were big up in Beacon, Fishkill, and places like that. So, I was in the offices by the four or five towns we provided cable to, and I noticed they were running a little black and white unmanned camera that panned back and forth, the Vidicon camera. The first shot you would see was an ad across the group plus the weather, and we would stop there and give the people enough time to read the weather. Then, we would go to a shot of a fish tank. There would be fish floating around, and then we would go over to the sports report, then to the news, and then it would start all over again. The graphics were very large and not created electronically. We didn't have that ability in those days. This was in the late 70s.

One day, I was there visiting our New York system. A guy named Howard was the general manager, a nice guy. None of the people running these cable operations had any concept of programming or commercials. They were engineers, guys who could hook up the cable system but had no programming sense at all. That was my contribution. I'm talking to Howard when there was a knock on the door. The receptionist says, "We're getting hundreds of calls." He said, "What's up?" She said, "The viewers are upset. One of the fish died and is floating upside down in the tank, and it looks awful." I couldn't believe my ears. People were watching that fish tank and reacting to it. I said to myself, *This is a gold mine if we play it straight. Let's put ads on this part.* Have the weather portion printed, and insert "The weather is brought to you by Smith Oldsmobile." If you could get people to watch a dead fish and get upset about it, then TV is the most powerful media ever devised!

We constructed a news operation and tested it in New Bedford. Joe was the one assigned to make this thing work. He came up with a very nice newscast. It was about that community for that community. I was a speaker at many national cable conferences, talking about how you made money by doing local programming with local advertising. We were really on fire. I got an ACE, the highest cable award. Then Ted Turner, a good friend of mine, came up with CNN. I don't think it had anything to do with what I did, but we had come up with Northwest Cable News, a twenty-four-hour news service for the Northwest. Joe Langhan did all the programming.

We were worried about getting programming for the Food Network when we first started. We hoped we could get enough to fill the hours. Of course, there were repeats. Some were shown in the morning and then at night, which is fine because not everybody is going to watch all day long. We have to show them something they'll enjoy.

As I said, we wanted to go public. There was no place to go in the newspaper business because everyone was shrinking down, selling off, getting rid of papers. We had to get more investment money in there, so either we grow or we die. They had a company worth $400 million but nowhere near that in cash.

In fact, I don't even think they knew at the time what the company was worth. So, happily all the cable partners peeled off. Every single deal went through and paid off. So, now we needed the money, the cash, and the stock. I wanted to use stock because it is the simplest and has the least tax obligation associated with it. If you use cash, somebody has to pay it back right away. How can you go public when one of your biggest entities is owned by eight or nine other people? Either you have to sell off your interest, or you have to sell off or buy theirs. We chose to buy them out. We negotiated with all of these guys and bought them out. We owned 100 percent of the Food Network and then went public. Wherever we went, we got acceptance.

I was in heaven. I realized how much money I had just made. Stop and think about it. I had thousands of shares in a privately owned company. You had to go through holy hell to get it evaluated, and you just couldn't go out and sell a share of stock; you had to get approval to sell it. Going public was the easiest solution.

My net worth that day was 50 percent more after we rang the closing bell. All our management was there at the New York Stock Exchange. Late that day our management stood up on the balcony by the big clock looking down on the floor at the people buying and selling shares, and then we closed the market. From that point on, I was a God-like creature. Those people were hugging me. I made them a lot of money. But fair enough, they gave me an opportunity, and I did well.

The biggest impediment with the Food Network was just getting it on cable. The cable companies, although we were all good friends, every one of them wanted to make a hard-nosed deal. It was my idea not to charge the cable operators for the first ten years. When the ten years were up, they all paid. It became one of the most popular networks ever.

We owned 100 percent of the Food Network. We went around the country, Trygve and I, negotiating the buyout of the other people.

It was a very significant moment in the history of that company. We now had money in the bank. Suddenly, I had more money than I ever dreamt of. I was happy with my salary, and I loved doing what I was doing. I was rich!

I was looking at more television stations along the coast. A station was available in Las Vegas, Channel 13. Las Vegas is one hell of a market. Now we had stock. So, I can give you $25 million worth of stock, and you can do with it what you want. If the stock goes up, who is coming out better? The thing is, if it goes down . . . but at the time we were doing this, it was going up every day. The pressure on the board of directors, which I was not aware of, from the shareholders of the Providence Journal Company, was that our little newspaper was now worth gazillions, and they would like to get the gazillions.

They were approached by Belo Corporation to merge. I knew Belo, and they were very successful. They had a bright new chairman, Robert Decherd, and he wanted to grow. Steve Hamblett, ProJo's CEO, was to the point where maybe it was time to cash in. By this time, Trygve Myhren had cashed in, sold, and left the company. The first thing we did was sell all of our cable operations to Continental Cablevision. We had 800,000 subscribers, and we made a stock deal.

Continental Cablevision went public by trading their company to U.S. West. In so doing, we got U.S. West stock, which we quickly got rid of. We were out of the cable business, which I didn't like. I would not have done any of this except the going public. I wanted to go public so I could have money to buy more properties, since I could not do it with my good looks. God knows that.

I was stunned by this. I thought it was awful. Belo gave us their stock, which was worth about one-third more than ours. They are nice people. Belo wanted to grow with their new management deal. I was asked to do the due diligence with them, so I took them around the country and introduced them to all of our properties.

Quietly, without telling me, the Providence Journal Company was negotiating to get rid of the whole company. That's where Scripps came back in. Scripps did not get the whole deal; they got the Food Network. Other people got other pieces. Ken Lowe of Scripps is a very remarkable young guy. He's the one who led that whole charge.

In one of the early cable meetings, Ken came over and said, "If you're ever going to sell the Food Network, call me first." I like him a lot, he's a very nice and smart guy. We have these meetings every few months. The last one, a year ago, Ken was the speaker along with the head of Nielsen. I said to Ken, "Can I buy the Food Network back?" and he said, "Yeah, for $9 billion."

I'm very proud of myself; I earned every single penny. No one gave me a handout, no one gave me anything. I did get love from my mother, father, and sister; my wife; my high school principal; and some other people along the way. I have done my best to share that attitude with college and high school students. You can do anything you want to do in this country today if you put your mind, heart, and soul behind it. God gave me the willingness to do that, and I have had a heck of a good time.

A Good Lawyer Knows the Law; A Great Lawyer Knows the Judge!

MIKE ISAACS

Mike Isaacs

Mike Isaacs is a former broadcasting, cable television, and media executive and current attorney in Rhode Island. In 2014, he was elected president of the Town Council in East Greenwich, Rhode Island, for a sixth term.

I first met Jack when I was working as assistant general counsel at the National Cable Television Association. That was 1980, when cable was just starting to expand out of rural into suburban areas. Jack had been hired by the Providence Journal to run their broadcasting and cable division, which really at the time consisted of two radio stations in Providence and a small cable system. They were competing against rival companies to get the cable TV license for different communities.

Jack recruited me to head the franchising activities of the Journal at that time. It was an exciting period. I was interested but somewhat reluctant because I was an attorney at the trade association. They had a lot of good contacts among Washington law firms. I really saw my career path as joining a law firm in Washington, if I ever left the trade association.

But Jack pointed out that I should be open to different kinds of opportunities, to something new, and not have a preconceived notion of what my career was going to look like. That was one of the best pieces of advice I was ever given, and I'm glad I took it. It was a great job, a great time period. It was the most fun job I've ever had.

We concentrated our franchising efforts primarily in New England, southern Florida, and southern California. I'd spend time going to communities and making presentations before city councils. On many of those trips, I'd travel with Jack. That was always a blast, especially given Jack's love of Mexican food. We always ate well. We always found great Mexican restaurants. When we started expanding in television, Jack bought TV stations in Tucson and Albuquerque. So that was really fun and exciting.

That was a terrific period to be in the cable television industry. It was entrepreneurial. It was competitive. We were out there. It was like a sporting event to some extent. We're competing against other companies. Then you move on to the next community, pretty much competing against the same people. We were building value. We were bringing a new kind of service to communities— cable television, new cable. Not all the new channels had come on yet during that period, but they were starting to. We really felt like we were part of something that was changing the face of television and entertainment and communication in the country.

The invention of the word processor allowed us to submit all these applications much more easily than if they had to be typed or printed the old-fashioned way. It allowed us to take existing documents and make minor changes to tailor them to a new community, so the turnaround time was very fast. The applications we submitted were like multivolume documents, explaining what we would do and highlighting the services we'd offer, talking about the company, the personnel.

Jack and I made a good team. One of the reasons we were successful was Jack's personality. When he met one on one with politicians, mayors, town council members, city council members, they all loved Jack. Jack's skills in the public presentations and his willingness as the CEO of the company to be there were vital. We could say, "Our CEO will give attention to this community. You'll have access to the head of the company when you need it. He'll be here when you need him." That was a big factor in our success.

We bought an independent station that then became the Fox affiliate in Tucson. Our license was actually in Nogales, which is a small town on the Mexican border. Our transmitter was there. There was some zoning issue, which I can't recall, but we needed permission from the Nogales City Council for zoning. What we needed to do was very important to us.

We got the approval. We went to this little bar in Nogales after the meeting to celebrate. Jack's looking at the menu. This is 1982, and they have Dom Perignon on the list. To celebrate, Jack orders a bottle of Dom Perignon. I don't think this bar in Nogales had served many bottles of Dom. The waitress comes, opens the bottle. You can tell she's a little nervous. This is the most expensive champagne they have. She drops the bottle on the floor and it shatters. The champagne's all over the place. Jack didn't want her to get in trouble. He was very gracious. He called the manager over and told him we were paying for it. It would have been probably her night's salary.

Our company was scrupulously honest, as were most, but some companies were not. During those days, you had some local businesspeople forming companies just to get the franchise with the sole intent of then reselling it.

The other thing that happened in those days in cable was that, in some areas, it became a practice to involve local businesspeople as part of the ownership group of a franchise. The typical deal would be maybe 10 percent ownership. Our deal was that they had to buy in. We didn't just give them their stock for free, but we lent them 100 percent of the money in a nonrecourse loan. It was really a "no lose" for them if we won the franchise.

We had a situation in Massachusetts where we lost a franchise. We had a superior bid. For one thing, in parts of southeastern Massachusetts, there's a large Portuguese population. And we had developed our own proprietary Portuguese language channel, where we bought programming from Portugal and Brazil and produced some programming. Our competitors didn't offer that, didn't have access to it.

In one area, a company whose proposal was not nearly as good as ours won the franchise. Jack was absolutely livid. The mayor's nephew was our lawyer. We called him. We demanded a meeting with the mayor. We wanted to know why we didn't get that franchise.

Jack and I, one of our local partners, and our lawyer went to meet with the mayor, and he's giving us all these reasons why we didn't get it, which were all BS. Finally, we're walking out of the meeting, and he turns to Jack and says, "You know, you should really be proud of your company and your people though. You're the only ones who didn't try to offer me something." I'm not sure if he had just made an incriminating statement about what influenced the outcome of his decision. We just looked at each other, but we knew something had probably gone down in that community.

Jack was terrific to work for as a boss because he let people do their job. He didn't micromanage. He expected results. He expected performance, but he let you do your job. He wanted to be kept informed, as one would expect. The other really good thing is you could tell him bad news. If there was bad news, he didn't immediately look for somebody to blame. I always felt comfortable.

Jack listened to people. It was clear that Jack was going to make decisions. We would have some heated discussions in our staff meetings. People were free to express their opinions, free to debate with him. But, in the end, as Jack said at one meeting, our version of democracy was that we all expressed our opinions. We all vote, and Jack decides. He was very good that way.

It was fun listening to Jack—traveling with him, too—the stories he told about the early days of television. Jack had some great stories from Arizona, from his time in Atlanta, working with Ted Turner before Ted became a cable television mogul. It was an interesting period. We just had good times together.

When I look back at that time period at the Providence Journal, Jack, almost in spite of the upper management and the board, transformed that company into a multimedia company with significant value. The management and the board of the parent company at that time were very provincial. Jack kept pushing and pushing to expand and move into these other areas and played a very significant role in that company being what it was at the time we went public and at the time of the sale, you know, of course along with Trygve Myhren. Trygve came from the outside. Without Trygve and Jack, that company would not have grown the way it did.

In traveling with Jack, his theory was to keep on the move. If there were delays or bad weather, Jack's idea was, "Let's find another close city to head out to so we can get on another plane and keep moving and maximize our chances of getting home." Jack approached business as keeping on the move and being on the offensive.

Two interesting instances came up on the television side. This was in the days of early independent television in the mid-to-late eighties. One involved the University of Arizona and our athletic contract, and the other was syndicated programming. In those days, we had a contract with the University of Arizona to carry their sports on our television station. During football season, our Tucson general manager calls Jack one day and tells him, "I just got a call from the athletic director at the university telling us that we're not going to be able to televise the home game this week because the Pac 10 is going to show that on their new cable network instead," you know, a pay network instead.

Jack was astonished. He called me in to be involved in the matter. He spoke to the general manager of the television station in Tucson. He said, "What's going on here?" We said, "You know, we looked at this contract. Nowhere in our contract does it say that they can just tell us you don't get to carry a game. We have a contractual right to carry."

City Councilwoman Joan Milke Flores awarding me the franchise for the Los Angeles Harbor cable area, 1987.

We got involved in conversations with the University of Arizona. They said, "Well, this is a Pac 10 rule." We came back and said, "Since when does the Pac 10 rule supersede the validity of our contract with you? There's a provision in the U. S. Constitution on breach of contract, and there are no amendments that gave the Pac 10 the right to override that."

Summer meeting of Colony Communications management, Newport, Rhode Island, mid-'80s. To the right of Jack is Bruce Clark, President.

We told them we had every intention of having our crews at this game. We were going to televise it, and if they prohibited us from doing that, then Jack said we would just run a blank screen with a continuous scroll that said, "While this game could have been brought to you on free over-the-air television, the University of Arizona has decided to prohibit us from carrying the game and therefore deprived its loyal alumni of the opportunity to watch this telecast."

The university and the Pac 10 went to court to try to get an injunction to prohibit us from carrying the game. It was a Saturday, hours before game time, when the judge held a telephone conference and ruled in our favor. Subsequently the case went to trial. We won at trial.

The other thing was the growth of independent television. Independent stations like ours lived by purchasing syndicated programming because we didn't have programming from the network. This was a period in which the FCC was granting new licenses for independent stations. We began to find out that stations that had come on the air after us were having financial troubles. Some of these stations would bid against us for programming, really outbid us, skewer the marketplace, and then go back to the syndicators who would give them deals to pay lower prices for what we did in the first place.

Obviously we thought this was really unfair. Jack always felt like, and our company felt like, we honored our agreements and were fair with people. People should be fair with us. Jack went back to the syndicators and basically said, "If you're giving deals to people, we'd like some deals, too," and their response was like, "Well, no. You're paying your bills." Basically, "You're good customers. You're paying your bills. So we're not going to—we're not doing this."

Jack told the managers of these television stations and said to me, "Well, that's fine. Stop paying their bill. You get a bill from these certain syndicators that are treating us this way, don't pay the bills." And Jack told them to refer the phone calls to me.

Sure enough, about sixty days later, we started getting the phone calls. "We're going to pull the programs. Your bills are overdue." We said, "Yeah, but you're giving breaks to everybody. We want in on this renegotiation." Eventually some accommodations were made. Interesting things happened in those periods in the way people dealt with each other.

When Providence Calls, Ya Gotta Accept the Challenge!

CHARLES MOCK

Charles Mock

Charles Mock is a former executive vice president for the Providence Journal Company (1969–2000) in the Human Resource Department and was instrumental in hiring Jack Clifford.

In 1977, I worked at the Providence Journal. We had the newspaper— which was the holding company— three commercial printing plants, and a couple of radio stations, and we were really going big time into cable television. A subsidiary of the Journal, Colony Communications, was the cable TV company. Our president there was about to retire. I needed to find somebody who could take over for him. We were thinking seriously about buying some TV stations.

I looked for the guy who could do all of this, and I found Jack. He was the perfect guy for the job. I met him a couple of times, and I went out to California and sat with Jack and his wife and hired him to become president of Colony Communications. He took that over, did a marvelous job, and got us into television. He found the first television station we bought, which was in Philadelphia. In the end, we had twelve television stations, all the way from Hawaii to North Carolina, and Jack was in charge of all of them.

Our cable television operation was in the top ten of the country. When the cellular telephone business was emerging, we decided to get into that, and Jack was in charge of it. He was in charge of everything that had to do with communications and just did a fantastic job.

Jack came to us one day and said, "I've been talking to a guy who is thinking about starting a program in the food industry." We said, "Gee, that sounds interesting." Jack started the Food Network. The last time I talked to Jack, he was very unhappy about it. He said, "Charlie, right now, the Food Network is worth more than the whole Belo Corporation" who bought the Journal when Jack retired.

Jack and I made the Providence Journal a lot of money. I give him great credit for it. He really was a hard worker and a very smart guy. I hired Jack because we had good chemistry. Jack knew the business. He'd been around. He knew the radio business, the cable business, and TV. He just seemed like the right guy.

I was there when Michael Metcalf was there. I think Metcalf's death was a mob deal. Metcalf was the principal owner of the company and the chairman of the board. Regardless of my title, I was his right-hand man. He was a man of integrity.

Since then, the Providence Journal has been sold twice, and it has declined noticeably. If Metcalf had been there and not been killed, I'm telling you, we probably would have been the largest cable TV operative in the country and the top cellular telephone company in the country because we were headed in that direction. We would have been one of the major communications companies in the United States.

We owned the WHAS television station in Louisville, Kentucky. We had access to the racetrack there, Churchill Downs, and had a lot of fun at the Kentucky Derby. The station broadcast some of the local college football games there, too. Jack tried to get me out in the middle of the field there one time during halftime. I fought him. I wouldn't do it. He was trying to promote WHAS.

We went down to the Masters a couple of times. We stayed in a hotel, and right next to us was Fuzzy Zoeller. He was a lot of fun. At the time, I was trying to hire a cartoonist from the *Augusta Chronicle*. I'd made him an offer to come to the Journal as an editorial cartoonist. Jack and I bumped into him, and I said, "Well, are you going to take our job?" He said, "No, but I've got to thank you from the bottom of my heart." I said, "What happened?" He said, "I told my boss I was going to the Providence Journal. He gave me a raise, doubled my pay, and did all kind of things to keep me."

A Hard Way to Make an Easy Living

PAUL McTEAR

Paul McTear

Paul McTear is president and CEO of Raycom Media. McTear is the former vice president of finance for the broadcast and media division of the Providence Journal.

I met Jack in 1978 when he came down to buy what was WPHL TV, Channel 17, an independent television station in Philadelphia. If my memory serves me correct, he paid $11 million for the television station, and the Providence Journal didn't put up a dime. They borrowed 100 percent of the purchase price from Chase Manhattan Bank. When the deal was done Jack visited the station and met with station management. This was ProJo's first TV acquisition, and Jack did not like the station operating plan for 1979. He asked us to redo the plan and said he would be back the next week to see what we came up with. He returned and disliked the new plan totally. I was the only one who challenged him. There was a long pause, and finally Jack smiled and said, "Paul you're right! I'm wrong! Let's work together on this." We did, and Jack a few years later told me he found a tough and honest man in me.

I had the good fortune to be at the first television station the Providence Journal ever bought. They recruited Jack to help balance their portfolio and to acquire television stations. They were a newspaper, a small-time cable operator, and an even smaller-time pager operator company, and they were interested in technology that could grow the newspaper they had owned since 1828.

That's where I met Jack. We began a relationship that lasted quite a long time. From, I guess, that budget meeting in late '78 through early 1997, I worked either indirectly or directly for Jack for most of those years. Working with Jack, we acquired television stations, first in Tucson and Albuquerque, obviously areas of the country Jack loved. They weren't great stations, but, you know, at least we had a foothold.

Then the Bingham family in Louisville, Kentucky, began fighting the father over the assets. They ended up selling all the businesses. They sold the newspaper and the television and radio stations. We were fortunate enough to win and own WHAS-TV in Louisville, which is a heritage television station.

WHAS-TV sponsorship of the fourth race of the Kentucky Derby at Churchill Downs.

When we first purchased WHAS, Jack was kind enough to invite my wife and I to attend the Kentucky Derby as a result of our ownership there. Jack and Marguerite fell in love with horses, maybe more so Marguerite than Jack. Marguerite was a kind, gentle, and generous person. She played the horses like we all did down there. We were two or five dollar bettors or whatever it is. She managed to win the Kentucky Derby every year. We finally found out that her success was due to the fact that she bought a ticket for every horse. If there were twenty horses running, she would quietly step out, get in line, buy twenty tickets, and then sit in the corner and scream and yell, "Oh, my goodness! I won! I won!"

I'm an accountant by trade. I was an accounting major, a business manager, etc., etc., but Jack never looked at me as being just an accountant, and he exposed me to everything and threw all kinds of ideas up against the wall. Some actually stuck.

One of the funnier parts of our lives together was when we went down and transitioned WHAS into the Providence Journal culture from the old Bingham family culture. Together he and I rented an apartment down the street from the TV station. We spent about a month or so where we actually lived together and cooked breakfast in the morning. Despite the difficulties of work, we always managed to have an abundance of laughs and good humor and were able to keep things light.

We bought Louisville, and then the Providence Journal decided to sell WPHL television because the Philadelphia market was very competitive. We were still an independent television station. They believed there was more downside than upside, so they sold it. Jack said, "Look, I'd like to keep working with you. I'd like to offer you an opportunity to move to Providence, Rhode Island."

In the mid-eighties, my family and I picked up and moved to Providence. I began working directly with Jack, not only on television but on cable work and some of the paging stuff, and by then we were in the cellular business as well. Jack had spread our interests around so that the electronic side of the house was really the most significant part. His stature and influence on the company really was growing.

Jack is listed as a member of the cellular pioneers. He and I organized P. J. Cellular, and off we went to Raleigh, North Carolina. That was our first cellular franchise and our second joint apartment. When the time was right, Jack made a recommendation to sell the cellular business. We went through a long process of diligence and sold out to GTE for ten times our investment.

Then we had an opportunity to buy King Broadcasting in Seattle. We closed on that deal in 1992. We met with Credit Suisse, which was First Boston at that time. First Boston introduced us to I guess what you would call a private equity fund in today's parlance, a firm down on Park Avenue in New York called Kelso. We were able to structure a deal whereby the Providence Journal and Kelso entered into a joint venture, created a partnership that enabled us to put up 50 percent of the equity. Kelso put up 50 percent of the equity, and First Boston put up the remainder of the cash, and we bought King Broadcasting, a family business headquartered in Seattle. We bought their five television stations and the cable TV operations with 200,000 subscribers. We ended up with an NBC station in Seattle, an NBC station in Portland, a CBS station in Spokane, an NBC station in Boise, and a TV station in Honolulu, KHNL-TV. That was a Fox station that ended up moving to NBC.

We had five new television stations to add to this little growing portfolio, if you will, of broadcast properties. We added at some point a second television station in Tucson, and we started a twenty-four-hour-a-day cable channel called Northwest Cable News by tying together King TV in Seattle and KGW in Portland, Spokane, and Boise. We believed there was a uniformity of culture and lifestyle in the Pacific Northwest. There was a commonality of interest.

If you compared it to the Northeast, the people in New York didn't really care what was going on in Boston and vice versa, but in the Pacific Northwest, there are a lot of similarities and a lot of families spread out. We used our retransmission negotiations to gain carriage and a slight fee structure to get that accomplished. That network is still on the air today. It used to be Belo, and it's now part of the Gannett organization.

Two other networks got built along that time. The folks over at Colony came to Jack with an idea of creating some food programming. The original thought was that they would have the College of Culinary Arts at Johnson & Wales University be part of this idea. Just as the ideas were being formulated, Johnson and Wales pulled out. Jack, the Colony guys, and I really had to sit down and design a new program.

They hired a guy named Reese Schonfeld who came from the start-up team at CNN to handle it. They started off on Third Avenue in a dark and gloomy place and thus began what today is the Food Network. We built a studio eventually on Sixth Avenue and started a business up there. One of the most startling pieces of its success is the way it was put together. At the time, retransmission was coming about, and television stations could use their retransmission rights to gain carriage and those kinds of things.

We put together an equity structure that enabled the Providence Journal and Jack Clifford to go to his good friend Jim Dowdle who ran the Tribune Company. The Tribune Company and the Providence Journal would use their retransmission rights to gain carriage for this start-up fledgling Food Network, and both Jack and others thought, "Well, you know, all the big cable guys have pieces of this and pieces of that. Why don't we get the middle guys, the middle cable operators, and get them involved and grant them equity for clearing some of this?"

At the end of the day, it was a unique, almost far-out idea to cobble together a distribution platform among middle cable operators and two broadcast companies to jump-start the Food Network. You look back on it today, and it's extraordinary where that simplistic idea has gone. I was in the Atlanta airport a few weeks ago, and there's a Food Network restaurant there.

We also partnered with some entrepreneurs who came to us to invest, and we launched the twenty-four-hour-a-day America's Health Network, out of a studio in Orlando, Florida, right next door to Nickelodeon. Between 1978 when I started there and 1997 when Jack and I left , when the business was sold, we went from one television station, a small cable business, a small paging business, and a newspaper to twelve television stations and three cable networks. We had built the cable business to over a million subscribers and sold it to Continental and then sold the paging business. We were in and out of the cellular business. In order to create value for the many shareholders, the younger generation, these very wealthy New England families, we took the company public in the summer of '96 in order to provide liquidity for these folks, and, at the same time, provide some basis of growth to the company. If Jack or others went in and tried to do a purchase, we had stock we could share with potential takeover targets.

As luck would have it, within a period of three or four months, Jack, I, and a handful of folks were called into the chairman of the board's office one Friday afternoon and told to go home and get a bag packed, go down to New York, and answer some due diligence questions because we just sold the business. I'll never forget this—"Don't worry about it. I'm going to be okay." That's what the chairman of the board told us.

It was very scary when I first heard about the Food Network. We were disciplined in two areas. We were disciplined from a distribution standpoint, and we were fairly frugal on the cost side of the business, but I'm telling you, revenue was very elusive. They decided we would not charge for distribution. We were a 100 percent advertising business. If you don't have fairly extensive distribution and if you don't have a lot of ratings, getting revenue is going to be a challenge. It was scary, and it was worrisome, but somehow or other, we stuck it out.

We had start-up costs in 1995, and the Food Network went on the air in 1996. We were losing a lot of money in those days. The difficulty is that, when it was sold to Belo in 1997, Jack and I and others associated with its formative years never got a chance to see it through. We had a vision of what it could be. But the folks at Belo got it along with some other businesses and assets that were part of our portfolio, and they didn't know what to do with it. They were a newspaper and television company, and anything that didn't fit in that box, they didn't quite understand. Perhaps it's better to say it wasn't as important to them.

So they entered into an agreement with the folks at Scripps and swapped their equity interest in the Food Network for KENS-TV in San Antonio and wrote Scripps a check. Scripps is the owner of it and was able to make that investment for a very good price, and now it's worth a tremendous amount of money.

I was at the Providence Journal when Mike Metcalf was still alive. Jack felt a personal allegiance to Mike. Jack was hired by Mike, and Jack believed it was Mike's goal to balance the Providence Journal Company. His death was extremely troubling to Jack and Marguerite. That led to Steve Hamblett being promoted and given the increased responsibility of running the businesses.

If they hadn't taken these measures, the Providence Journal Company would have been bought out in a different way. The *Providence Journal* newspaper was part of the assets purchased by Belo back in 1997, and you probably know they've since put that asset up for sale. If it wasn't for the television business and the expansion into these cable businesses, I don't believe the value received by the shareholders in 1997 would have been anywhere near as significant as it turned out to be.

Jack and I parted business ways in February of 1997, but our friendship remains. Today I run Raycom Media, a company with 4,000 employees. We run fifty-some television stations and have a bunch of investments outside of the television business. I've been given any number of awards by *Broadcasting & Cable* magazine, the Broadcast Hall of Fame, and other accolades through the success of Raycom Media. I would tell you that I owe an awful large part of it to Jack Clifford, and it goes back to my very earliest days with him.

Jack never pigeonholed me by saying, "You're just an accountant." He allowed me to do and to succeed and, more importantly, to make mistakes and to grow as a result of those mistakes. It doesn't mean that, from time to time, I didn't get a good ass chewing, but Jack was always there the next day or a half hour later to brainstorm another idea or discuss something equally foolish, and I mean that. No matter where I go, I will tell anybody anywhere that a large part of who I am today is because of Jack Clifford, and I'll never forget that. Jack Clifford was as unselfish a leader as anybody I've ever had the privilege of working for. I will always be grateful to Jack.

Jack Clifford Is the Most, To Say the Least

PAUL ST. ONGE

Paul St. Onge is a financial planner and holds an MBA from Bryant University. He manages over $150 million for more than fifty families.

Paul St. Onge

I was introduced to Jack by one of his employees, a business associate of his, in the mid-nineties. He was at the Providence Journal at the time.

When I met Jack, he needed some financial counseling. We met, and we developed a business relationship that's lasted until now. Since I've met him, we've done many things together, many different investments, many different activities. We've had a very fruitful relationship. It's been very successful financially and we became very close friends.

Probably the most memorable transaction we had was an investment brought to us by the former CFO of the Providence Journal Company. The CFO, a relatively young guy, had left the company and decided to become a venture capitalist. He brought an opportunity to Jack that I had looked at first. Jack and I reviewed it and were very skeptical. We weren't convinced it was something we wanted to do, but Jack, being the kind of person he is, made an investment in this company just because he wanted to do a favor. He wanted to help him out, so he made a $100,000 investment. This became the greatest investment of Jack's life. That $100,000 blossomed into tens of millions of dollars and was our most memorable transaction. We've had others that didn't work out, of course, but the kind of guy Jack was and is, it's really the moral of the story because he's helped so many people through the years.

Jack is probably the finest overall person I have ever met. He's a wonderful, wonderful man. He's a people person. That's his approach with me, and I've seen his approach with people who work for him. He's got just a great understanding of how to treat people. He's an outstanding, fantastic, very emotional, very good person.

Chapter 5

The Food Network
Take This Job and Love It

Rich Wolfe

The founding of what is now the Food Network was Joe Langhan and my brainchild. I thought to myself, *Would people be interested in a food program?* Joe was the head of Colony Cable's local programming, and I was Colony's CEO and VP at ProJo. Joe told me that Johnson & Wales University's College of Culinary Arts, headquartered in Providence, was interested in producing a thirty-minute show teaching people how to cook. The show was to run on Colony systems serving Providence, Rhode Island, and New Bedford, and Fairhaven, Massachusetts. Joe and I had a meeting with J&W management a few days later, and by that time I saw this thing not as a local show but as a national network.

J&W backed away due to cost, but Joe and I and my staff director for business development, Andrew Thatcher, got excited and made a presentation to my boss Trygve Myhren, president of ProJo, who bought the idea. He assigned me to head up the project. Joe in turn encouraged me to hire Reese Schonfeld on a consulting basis to research the potential of the Food Network. Now, Reese Schonfeld helped Ted Turner create CNN. I knew Reese personally because he was with United Press International. He called on television and radio stations and encouraged them to take the United Press International wire service for their news operations. Reese and Joe got me the facts. Reese was so excited about what he came back with that he wanted to invest. He said the cable operators wanted it, and the public wanted it. He thought it was going to be huge. He and his wife, Pat, found a studio on Third Avenue in the heart of New York City and we began to move ahead with the new network. I asked Reese to be the network's president and Paul McTear to be the CFO. I became the chairman and CEO.

Trygve was very much part of convincing ProJo that this could be successful. With his background and respect in the industry, he helped bring key people to the table. We made joint presentations, with Reese, to potential investors. We were getting there without Trygve, but it would have taken a lot longer and been more work if he hadn't been on board. I was the primary mover and shaker at the Food Network. Trygve had other interests in the company to tend to—the newspaper, cellular, and all that—but he was always there for me. I don't remember us ever having an argument.

Trygve graduated from Dartmouth and had been in cable television for a long time. When I got to know him, he was working for the largest cable operation at that time, ATC, out of Denver. He's one of the nicest guys you'll ever know. If there was ever a boss I would have died for, it was Trygve Myhren. He was so good to me. He listened to me. I had to convince him, but once convinced, he was in all the way. I haven't always had the privilege of working with someone who profoundly believed in what I was doing.

My job was to put together the investment side to pay for this. The Food Network show was not my idea—it was Joe Langhan's—but I came up with the idea of the network. Reese and I pounded the pavement, and we got nine partners. Cable companies all liked me, knew me, and respected me, but not all wanted to do this deal. Some of them now are knocking their heads on the floor, but that's their problem. The biggest cable operator of all in those days, John Malone, turned it down, but eventually they had to come along. The first cable company we went after was Comcast in Philadelphia. They didn't see programming as important. Boy, did they later change their mind. They had no interest in it at the start though. That was disappointing because I thought they would join for sure.

I have forgotten the fine details, but roughly for every thousand subscribers cable companies had, they got additional shares of stock. We all put in $10 million, which came to $100 million. Jim Dowdle was the CEO of the Chicago Tribune Company. He was willing to give the Food Network the Tribune's retransmission rights.

In return, the cable companies gave the Food Network a channel. The Tribune received an ownership in the Food Network equivalent to the subscribers we achieved that way. Anyway, the deal was that we'd have ten of us own it, and I would be the general partner. I put together a management team. We did production.

Our first task after obtaining the ten investing partners was to acquire coverage on cable systems. Cathy Rasenberger, Michael Isaacs, and I set out together to sell the Food Network to cable operators. Cathy was the former key affiliate salesperson for ESPN. She came on board as our affiliate director. Colony hired Michael Isaacs, an attorney who worked for the state of

Massachusetts regarding cable TV activity. It was not an easy task. But we persevered. It became apparent that we would have to find a unique way to encourage cable operators to carry our program service. It was decided that for the first ten years of carriage, the cable operator would pay nothing to the Food Network for the service. We would survive on advertising revenue alone.

Remember, most of the cable was either owned by entrepreneurs who thought they knew more than anybody else in the world or by technicians who only really believed in putting wires in people's homes. Then along came the satellite. Cable operators saw this thing as a potential divider. We could not give the Food Network to them exclusively; that was against the law. Anything that was on cable had to be made available to satellite.

I had the advantage of being in on the origin of the satellite business. I was president and general manager of NBC affiliate KTAR in Phoenix then. It had been owned by the local newspaper, so KTAR stood for Keep Taking the Arizona Republic. The satellite was up there at that time. Every one of the three major networks had affiliates. The affiliate bodies would meet every year and negotiate contracts with the networks. The networks would pay us for our program time, but first they would reduce what they paid us by deducting the cost of interconnection. We all thought we were being taken advantage of and thought if we could get around that and have it all go on satellite, it would be a lot cheaper. Plus we would get more money out of our investment.

We formed the Phoenix Satellite Corporation and made the first application for a nonmilitary receiver for satellite information. We were granted the right and were going to put it up by South Mountain. There was not a tree within a hundred miles of that place, up that high, so we had a clear shot at that satellite. This disturbed the networks considerably. We never did put the satellite dish up. We were going to have one satellite dish with the capacity to have all three networks delivered to that dish and then taken individually to their proper affiliate.

By the time my staff and I had completed an investment plan and a sample program schedule for what was to become TVFN (Television Food Network) we had to rush to announce the idea at the Western Cable Show in San Francisco. We were too late to get a lunch or dinner spot so we set up a breakfast and invited the cable operators. Only a few low-level cable staffers showed up! My staff (Joe Langhan and a few others) greeted this uninspiring turnout and wondered if we should cancel the pitch. I told them we were going to give the best presentation these few guests had ever seen. It worked because at the end of the convention word got out that "Clifford's gang had come up with a unique idea!" At the following year's Western Show, we had a standing-room-only turnout.

I had such faith in Joe. To this day I think he's one of the best producers in television, and he and I set out to create this food thing. Everything I asked him to do, he did. He was shy around what he considered important people, but he did his work. He made beautiful TV. He was able to do that when maybe some other guys couldn't. Joe produced a pilot. It was about three minutes but very professional, top-grade.

You have to remember that cable at that time offered viewers only maybe twenty channels. The problem with cable in the early days was that every few years they came out with another piece of equipment, from Sylvania or RCA, that expanded the number of channels we could put on the single service. One year it was ten, the next it was twenty, and then it was thirty. Those things cost a lot of money. Every mile, you had to put another box up there on the wire, and subscribers had to have a box in the home. You paid the boxes off by charging people a monthly fee for the service. Part of that fee went against owning the box, which cost us $100 or more, and part of it was for the service itself. It worked. You had to have staying power.

We did the Food Network because I wanted to be on the side of the product that made all the money. We were able to keep all that money. We had to pay the guy with the transponders and pay the people who owned the satellites, but to try to get on the coaxial cables was impossible. The networks had it all tied up.

Now back to Ted Turner. Thanks to his understanding, he was the first guy to go up on the satellites. He made that practical. Ted Turner and his belief in the satellite delivery of signals and the people at Home Box Office came around to cable operators like me and said they would give us the receiver dish, but they would take the cost of the dish from the fees we paid them. You don't get anything for the service until you pay for the dish. They gave us a $25,000 dish, we charged $9.95 per month for the service, and as soon as we got enough $9.95s to pay them back for the dish, it was ours free.

We built our first dish in Woburn, northwest of Boston. In those days, it was a ten-meter dish, practically as big as a house. That was the only way you could get satellite service. There were no high-powered satellites at that point. We had to have a big dish to get the low-power satellites' signal. The day we opened that thing up, we had everybody from HBO standing there gawking at this huge thing. It looked like a scene out of a science fiction movie. Shortly after that, the dishes shrank.

As I said, for the first ten years, we gave the Food Network to cable operators for free. We didn't charge them, but they could charge their subscribers. The day the Food Network started its eleventh year, they had to pay us $1.20 per subscriber per year. Multiply that by a hundred million for what the network was getting annually.

The Food Network has a broad reach. Who can argue with it? I wanted a network that was clean and decent that everybody could watch, whether you were five, fifty-five, or 105. There is no swearing. There is no nudity. There is no sexual suggestion. It's just fun with food on that network. Anybody with their family can watch and not be ashamed of what they are watching. How many other networks can you say that about? CNN I guess. Fox News. Stop and think about it.

Remember, I was born in 1933. I grew up on radio. We'd all sit around and watch that radio. It was the size of a refrigerator. There was a little window with a light behind it, which is how you knew what frequency you were on. It had a great big speaker. Jack Benny never said a foul word, but he was funny, as funny as could be. Some of his stuff still seems hilarious. Jack Benny, Don Wilson, and Eddie "Rochester" Anderson were a scream.

There never was a time when the Food Network was not going to happen. I was going to put that son of a gun on cable or die trying. I was taking all of our chips and throwing them in the pot. The meeting with Proctor & Gamble was big. That was really when I thought, *Hey, we have to do this. Nothing is going to stop us now.*

When the man said, "I've heard enough," I thought we were going to be let out of Proctor & Gamble. But then he says, "I'm going to give you $500,000." So we had $500,000 from the toughest in the business of advertising with about five minutes of presentation. If Proctor & Gamble would have said no, the next prospect would have been General Foods. We would have kept trying.

We started off, and all of a sudden everybody's talking about the Food Network. Restaurants were calling. Initially, we couldn't get any of the top chefs except Jacques Pepin. He was the only chef willing to go on. Then all of a sudden the top chefs realized they had to be on. We found this little guy by the name of Emeril Lagasse in Fall River, about thirty miles from Providence. He had two restaurants down in New Orleans and a couple of them in New England. We put him on the air, and he was terrible— absolutely awful—because he was in an empty studio with nothing but cameras. Fortunately, when I was in college, I ran an all-night radio show with a microphone and an empty studio. I realized you had to believe that that microphone or camera was a person. They were the people watching and listening. He never could do that. Most people can, but he couldn't. Reese came up with the idea of putting him in front of a live audience to see what would happen, and that did it. Then he became really cute and successful very fast.

We recruited the audience for our shows just like they do now. We sent people tickets and they'd come. It was a lot of fun. The first year Emeril was on he became one of the top ten talents on television. The first year! We didn't have to pay him very much in those days, but he sure made it big after that. You know, I was glad when he was paid $55 million by—who's the gal?— Martha Stewart.

Emeril is a very nice guy. The one thing you have to understand is that the talent makes it. If you don't have people with talent, you haven't got anything. We had all live programming. Now it's pretaped. In those days we'd just go from one set to another. We had three sets—this corner was Emeril's, this corner was so and so's.

We went on the air Thanksgiving week in 1993. We needed show ideas. My concept was that we were going to teach people how to cook and have some fun at the same time. We'd teach children how to cook; we'd teach single people how to cook. We'd teach everybody how to make roast beef—simple things—but we'd also do some sophisticated cooking. It wasn't going to be one of these things like Julia Child. Her problem was she was a French cook with very complicated recipes. She was interested in joining us but never did, although I darn near convinced her to join our board of directors at the Food Network.

In the early days of the Food Network an engineer inserted a porn film by mistake in the middle of a show. Our engineers would send the signal up to the satellite, and then it was relayed down to all of the TV stations. Everything was put on videotape. There were no live shows. They were videotaped and played back that night. Apparently, the engineer on duty was watching porn and hit the wrong switch. Instead of sending out whatever the show was, let's say *Emeril,* he sent out pornographic material for ten or fifteen minutes. It caused horrific ripples. It was a stupid mistake, but it wasn't malicious. We had to apologize to the FCC and face the music on that one.

I realized the Food Network was a success when we got 20 million subscribers signed, about three or four years into it. We got there fairly rapidly. You see, the overnight ratings, which were how you sold national advertising, were a big deal. You had to have 20 million, be in front of 20 million homes, before you got rated. So we got there fairly quickly, after starting with two hundred thousand. People were demanding their cable companies put the Food Network on their local systems.

Al Ruff was the head of engineering. Al was a talented broadcast engineer. He came to me one day and asked if I was familiar with the Internet. I told him no, but I was familiar with the computer and I could program things. I asked what the Internet was. He told me the Internet was being used by the military for information distribution, and it was going to be made available to the general public—not the information but the system. I told him I was enthusiastic about the computer and that we should look into it.

He came back and told me that for very little money, we could have our website now. He explained to me that it was a loose arrangement of millions of computers. I thought it was a pretty good idea, but I did not quite comprehend it as well as he did. He was very excited about this.

The Food Network was up and operating with 200,000 subscribers, and suddenly we are flooded with requests for recipes. Now, how the heck are we going to get the recipes to these people without breaking the back of the network? We would have to hire a staff just to lick the envelopes! Let's go back and give Joe Langhan another pat on the back. Joe said, "Jack, why don't we use the Internet?" I thought that was a heck of an idea and wanted to see how many people responded to that. They would have to know what the Internet was in order to get the recipes.

We told them to go to the website foodnetwork.tv to get recipes. Joe helped design the website, back when there were few websites. We immediately got hit by a hailstorm of Internet requests for recipes. All they had to do was go to the library and hook up to the Internet, which is what many did.

I also saw a way to make money on the Internet. I said, "Why can't we sell cookbooks, pots and pans, trips, or whatever?" We had a network with a large audience and told them to go to our Internet site and buy things, and they did.

The first product was cookbooks. I don't remember the first cookbook, but I thought, *Let's get going here.* Everything I touched during that time paid off. I batted 1,000, but I had a lot of help. Some of the ideas that did work out I was hesitant about. I don't want to take credit for somebody else's work or ideas. But I was willing to go to bat with a lot of these ideas. That Internet recipe idea was one of the big hitters for us; it saved us thousands of dollars, and it expanded our audience. We even sold clothes—kitchen and barbecue aprons. You had to find companies that would do that for you. We used fulfillment companies and paid them a fee to do it. All we had to do was distribute to the fulfillment company the data, and they would send out the apron, shirt, pressure cooker, or whatever it was. They took a percentage and we took the rest.

I had an idea and a vision. I wanted to be the best. I wanted food, and I got it. The research on food is so substantially positive it almost knocks you off your feet. Everybody eats, and everybody loves food. What do we do when a baby is born? We celebrate and have food. What do we do when the old boy dies a hundred years later? We celebrate and have food. We celebrate lives.

Everybody from the first gurgle to the last gasp celebrates with food and drink, not ping-pong balls, not mowing yards, it's food and drink. Our ancient brain still remembers how tough it was to get food. Remember that in primitive times when people were living in trees, when Papa came home with an elk, they all went bananas. Everybody descended on the elk, and we're still doing that in our own small way.

Joe Langham brought a great idea: hire Robin Leach. We had a cable show convention up in New York City around this time when we decided to announce the debut of the network. Robin Leach was there. He had a big coffee table book about his show *The Lifestyles of the Rich and Famous*. These cable operators are all guys, most of them rural-type individuals with little companies that had strung cable out in the boondocks somewhere. They were lined up for blocks to meet Robin Leach. I thought, *God I wouldn't go across the street to see this guy*, and I didn't. But I was wrong. Robin and I became pretty damn good friends.

Robin Leach came to the eastern show and announced that we were going to do the Food Network. These were cable operators, most of whom were engineers and construction people or guys who repaired radios. There were a few broadcasters like me, a few entertainers and so on, but most of these guys built cable from the ground up. "I got the signal" was their biggest triumph.

When I was first introduced to Robin Leach, I thought he was a wild man. I was a little worried about him, which I shouldn't have been because he proved to be a good guy. We go to this convention and there's a line, it looked like about a half mile of these engineer types waiting to get Robin's autograph and latest book. That said something to me. These are men now, not ladies; they are not socialites, they are just guys who build cable systems. They could not wait to shake the hand of Robin Leach. I thought, *Jack, wake up! This guy is popular.* I waited in line too, talking to people.

One time we were meeting in New Orleans. My staff—about ten of us—always got together and had dinner one night. Down comes Robin Leach with this group of women. They were all attractive, high worth. A couple of them were six feet tall and built like, you know. I watched this parade come into the dining room and just about passed out. He was just that way. He had to have more energy than any human being ever. We are trying to present a family-oriented panel here, and Robin shows up with all these ladies. I went up to his side and said, "Get them out of there. I don't care what you do on your own time, but get them out of here. Get them out of this hotel. They're gone or you're gone." And he said, "Okay, okay."

But Robin worked his tail off for us. He went to every meeting, every event where we needed support for the sales pitch. The first month all we had on was Robin Leach having Thanksgiving dinner with all his friends, and that led to other ideas. There are a billion ideas you can do with food. We had other chefs then that would come on. One thing just kept piling up on top of another. Look at it now.

Robin and I got along well. He was hardly the type you might think he'd be. He was very nice to us guys. He and I made presentations together convincing cable operators that this thing was going to be successful. He was always willing to help. Langhan and Reese made a good hire with Robin Leach.

Another early program that worked well was with Debbi Fields of Mrs. Fields Cookies. She was a beautiful, novel girl—absolutely stunning. Her program, however, was produced independently of our company, out of California. Her show was about desserts— she was the dessert queen. She was and is excellent. Her show lasted about three years. She was a joy to watch because she is so pretty, knowledgeable, and relaxed. We paid her for appearances. Her show was heavily sponsored. She was using Pillsbury dough and all, and they were all there. We did not having any trouble selling that.

Donna Hanover was a very fine actress, very nice. She was on our newscast, which did not work. It was called *News and Views From the World of Food.* It was not that she failed; it just was not of interest to enough people. It was because people like to watch other people cook food and try to do it in a distinctive way. If you are a hamburger fan, there are at least a half dozen channels where the stars of those shows are demonstrating a new way to serve hamburgers.

An amazing number of men watch the Food Network. I thought they would watch, but not that many. But everyone watches it. We have a huge children's audience. My granddaughters and grandsons, when they were about ten, watched the Food Network. It is a healthy network with decent images on the air. You can set your four-year-old down, and he is not going to see somebody shot. They have managed to maintain a standard of decency on that network, and I'm proud of it. I watch the Food Network and never get disappointed.

Food Channel Fever?
There's No Cure!

JOE LANGHAN

Joe Langhan serves as executive producer of the Wine Network. Mr. Langhan was one of the key players in developing the concept of the Food Network while at the Providence Journal Company in 1991. As vice president of production at the Food Network, he personally created many of the network's most successful programs, including Emeril Live *with Emeril Lagasse and* Cooking Live *with Sara Moulton. Prior to the Food Network, he created several regional cable networks, including a Portuguese-language channel in New England, a Spanish-language channel in Florida, and five regional news channels around the United States.*

I worked for Colony Communications, which Jack was in charge of. He was chairman of the broadcast and cable company. I had been working for him for quite a few years when ProJo decided they wanted to get into the cable network business. They wanted to come up with an idea for a network. Their criteria were unusual. One was that it had to be a subject matter popular in other mediums, such as magazines, but not available on television yet. The second was that it had to be something that could be 100 percent advertising supported. It had to be a category where a lot of money was being spent to advertise. The third thing is, they wanted to offer it to cable operators for no charge, no subscriber fee.

Marketing ended up spending about eight months coming up with a whole bunch of ideas, all of which were rejected, not by other people but by me. The ideas all had something going for them, but they didn't meet all the criteria the company was looking for at the time.

One day, I was in the office, and Jeff Wayne, who was head of marketing for the cable company, asked if I could meet with Ken Levy, who was the vice president of business development for

Johnson & Wales' College of Culinary Arts. Ken wanted to come in and get some advice on starting up a communication school within the university.

I was asking him a little about the school, which was right down the street from our office. I said, "I see all these people walking around with these white suits and chef hats on." He said, "Oh, yeah, we're the largest culinary school in the world in terms of numbers of students."

Anyway, he asked me about the communication school, and I told him I didn't think that was a good idea. I said, "Why would you want to do that?" He said he could get students in the communication school to videotape the cooking classes in the cooking school. I said, "Is it that important to tape these classes so that students who were sick that day could watch them?"

He said, "No, no, no. We could tape the classes and show them on the Interconnect channels." The Providence Journal had the right to program three channels that went all through the state of Rhode Island, called the Interconnect channels. We had a service there, JTV, which Jack was responsible for, too.

Jack had this idea for a movie channel, which was ahead of its time. It was called Movie Time. Because of Jack's TV programming, sales, and management background, we were looking around for ideas to put together channels. It was before there were a large number of national cable networks available. We had to create some of our own material. That's what I worked on for the company. We did channels in Portuguese and Spanish. We did local news channels and other things.

Jack says, "What would be really popular is putting together a movie channel," just movies, twenty-four hours a day, seven days a week. What was odd was that it was going to be advertising supported and these would be old movies.

We put this together just for the local area, Rhode Island and Massachusetts. It became popular pretty fast. I remember thinking this would be a good national cable network, but, for various reasons, it never got beyond the Rhode Island, southeastern Massachusetts area. This was before Turner Movie Classics (TMC) and before Chuck Dolan's Cablevision put together AMC.

That was the first "network" the company put together while

fooling around with the concept. The other thing, back in 1991, was that it had to be a proven audience concept. The cost for the programming had to be predictable and manageable.

At that time, these criteria weren't easy to meet. For example, the movie channel would have met two of those criteria, but the cost of buying the movies would have been pretty high. In fact, the only reason Ted Turner was able to do TMC is because he bought a studio with a library that had thousands of movies.

There were concepts like talk show channels, pet channels, and all kinds of ideas. After Ken Levy of Johnson & Wales told me we could put the programming on the Interconnect channels, I remember looking at him and saying, "But Ken, but who would watch that?" He said, "Well, my wife and I like to watch cooking shows, but we can only watch them on Saturday or Sunday on PBS." There were a few cooking shows at that time on the Discovery Channel and other cable networks, but not very many.

Within the following week or so, I started just anecdotally talking to people about cooking shows, and I was surprised to find out how many people I knew actually watched them. There was this one guy in particular, a friend of mine, who was the last person in the world I would ever think would watch a cooking show. He watched a show about Bayou cooking with a Louisiana guy, and it was being carried on PBS.

The idea of the cooking thing sort of came out of that. I went to Paul Silva, my boss, and Paul said, "You've got to write this thing up." So I went back and wrote it up as best I could at that time. Then he said, "All right. We'll go talk to Bruce." We went to Bruce Clark, president of Colony, and Bruce said, "So you think this is a good idea?" and Paul and I said yeah. It was the best idea we'd been able to accomplish over eight months. He said, "All right. Let me call Jack. We'll take it over to him."

At that point, we weren't that secure about the idea because none of us really watched cooking shows. None of us really cooked. But Jack saw the wisdom of the idea right away. Jack was pretty big into making bread and chili. He understood the concept a lot better than we did because of his personal involvement. Jack understood how many different people would have an interest in it because, until we talked to him, it was still in my mind more or less a women's channel. I didn't think it could get any bigger than that, which doesn't mean it wouldn't have been a good thing. We certainly weren't thinking about it being as big as it actually became.

Jack said, "Okay, I want you to do this, this, and that to flesh out the idea and do some more work on it." We did some more work on it, and then he took it to Trygve Myhren who was the president of the whole Journal company. Jack had to basically sell the idea to Trygve. My experience with Jack is that if he believes in an idea, he's the guy you want to sell it because he's probably the best salesman I've ever met. He knows how to present something.

We put it together the way Jack wanted it put together. Once Trygve thought the idea was worthwhile, he said, "We don't know how to put a network together. We've got to go out and find somebody who does."

Paul McTear was Jack's right-hand man at that time. Jack probably said, "Here's what I want you to do, and then I want you to run it by Paul and let him take a look at it before we take it any further." Paul got involved in it, too, at that time, right after Jack approved the whole thing.

We all called it the Cooking Channel, and, as it turned out, that was much too narrow a way to think about it. Jack came up with the name of "The TV Food Network." The concept broadened into food.

I'll tell you how this stuff works. First you're looking around for the right fit for the slot you're trying to fill. I don't care whether it's a program or a channel or a network or whatever. And then when you think you have the right concept, you have to immediately question it. You say, "Okay, yeah, it's a good idea, but will people advertise on it?" Then you do a little bit of discussion and research about that. You find out there's a lot of food advertising. Then you say, "Well, will people watch it?" Then you talk to a few people, and they say, "Yeah, cooking shows are pretty popular."

You go through each one of these steps and validate the idea, one step at a time. With a lot of ideas you go through one or two steps, and then, all of a sudden, you run into negativity or pushback on it. Then you say, "Well, that idea's not going to work."

But with the food thing, it was like every step of the way, everything became more and more positive. As that happens, you become much more committed to the concept. Think of it like this: if I come to you with an idea for something, and you've never thought or heard of the idea before, you naturally have a lot of questions about it.

After you work on an idea for a while and you keep going to more and more people, the circle of people keeps widening. Every time you talk to a new person, it's like you're starting back from the first step. Even when people react negatively about an idea, you quickly realize that the reason they're so negative about it is because they don't understand it. They don't know all that I know. So my job is to bring them up to speed on it, so to speak.

After you've done that, if they're still negative on it, then you have to figure out, "Why are they negative but I'm not? Is there something wrong with me? Is there something wrong about the way I'm thinking about it?"

Once you get a certain, I don't know what you call it, but a certain distance into something like this, you become the world's leading expert on the idea. As we went along, somebody being negative about the idea never really affected me unless the person was negative because he or she knew something I didn't.

What you have to do is basically be prepared for that "but." We spent a year and a half going into meetings where people would say, "but, but, but. I don't think this. You're not going to be able to produce those shows for that much money! It's going to cost three times that much!"

Each time somebody brings up a new "but," you have to go back. You have to work on it. You have to verify whether that's in fact true, whether it's a problem, and sort it out. Then you go ahead and go forward again. But the next time somebody brings up that "but," you say, "Okay, we've got that figured out. Here's the production plan. Here's the production budget. What do you want?"

For example, very late in the process, right before Jack decided to actually launch the channel, the Tribune Company got involved. George Babbitt worked for the Tribune at that time. He was the point guy at the Tribune Company who was helping to sell the idea to them. He and I worked together at the Food Network after the launch. When I got to know him later, he said Jim Dowdle, the Tribune CEO, took the plan for the Food Network and sent it to his production company within their TV division. He said, "Here's this plan. Tell me what you think of it."

Production sent back a memo saying, "The absolutely, positively lowest cost you can produce a cooking show for is $15,000." Our plan said we could produce them for $2,500 or $3,000. Remember, Jim Dowdle finally approved the Tribune's involvement. In an indirect way, Jim Dowdle basically rejected what his production company told him. The Tribune involvement was really what made the channel—it would not have happened if they didn't come in at that last moment.

Do you know what the biggest objection was? After Jack's presentation, they'd say, "If this is such a good idea, how come no one else is doing it?" It's funny. After the first two times I heard that, we talked to each other about it. I used to say, "How do you answer a question like that? If that's the objection, what's the answer to that?"

You can say that about everything new at some particular point—radio, television, cable television. You could say that about the steam engine. At some point, somebody was sitting there saying, "Gee, I can make this work, but why isn't anybody else doing it?" The answer we finally came up with was something along the lines of "Well, we don't know, but we're going to do it."

The other thing you run into is people within the organization whom you're trying to take in as a partner seeing conflicts with something else they want to do. They think up reasons why this is a bad idea. But they're really not necessarily believing that, they're just trying to protect their own interests.

There was a woman at Time Warner. We found out later she was trying to put together a lifestyle channel. She said, "Food is too narrow a category." She said it would only work if it was part of a channel that also had home decorating and blah, blah, blah. She knew what she was saying was hogwash. Time Warner never did invest in her channel concept.

When we started working on putting together the network, we did a lot of basic research. One time we locked ourselves in an apartment for three days and watched 250 cooking shows. We got tapes from all over the place, anybody who'd ever done a cooking show. We even had tapes from little TV stations in the Midwest. There was one show called *Kill It and Grill It*. It was a half-hour show. The first fifteen minutes was the hunt of something, and the last fifteen minutes was the cooking. That's just to give you an idea of all the different things that were actually out there, once we went out and looked for them.

Anyway, one of the shows we saw when we started watching all these things was a Thanksgiving special by Martha Stewart done with PBS. She had done that in 1989, and we were looking at it in 1993. She really wasn't a television star at that time. She had published a couple of books but had no magazine yet.

I saw that Thanksgiving Day special, and it impressed me, after watching all these other types of shows. So I watched it over and over again and took notes to try to figure out what was so good about it. Also I found out that it was popular. When I started asking people, especially women, I said, "I was watching this Martha Stewart," and they'd say, "Oh, Martha Stewart's great." I said, "Where did you see her?" They said, "She did this Thanksgiving thing where she did pumpkin soup, and she did this and did that."

Then I realized this Martha Stewart is a hot property, but she was too expensive for us to work with at that time. She was already getting too big. She had the books. She was starting to work with PBS on TV shows. At that time, anybody who was on PBS was getting paid about five times as much as we were willing to pay. That was not realistic.

But I did study the show. My coworkers started joking around, saying, "Oh, Joe has a crush on Martha Stewart." I said, "No, no. She's just really good at this. You ought to pay attention. Here's the tape. You ought to go watch it." One day, one of the producers in charge of booking guests on the show comes in and says, "Joe, we've finally done it." I said, "What's that?" She said, "We booked Martha Stewart to be on the network." I said, "Really? She's agreed to come on?"

She agreed. She came in to be on Robin Leach's show. The night we were doing the show, they told her, "Our head of production wants to meet you. He talks about you all the time." She came in. I said hello. She just laughed about it a little bit. I said, "I suppose they've been telling you how often I use your name, but it's not in vain or anything like that." She just laughed, and that was it.

Jeff Wayne and I worked together pretty closely. We had worked together for years. He was involved in the whole thing along the way and was up to date on what was happening. In any case, after the network actually got approved and it was obvious it was going to launch, we sat down and thought about it. We realized the network as a project had actually died nine times.

Then we went to the NCTA convention in Dallas, which was usually in May, maybe early June. We had what we thought was yet another meeting about the Food Network. Trygve and Jack dragged all these guys from the other cable companies that we had been talking to. There were nine of them all together.

They brought them together in the convention area for a breakfast meeting. Jack said, "Well, we want to talk about the Food Network." Some of the guys in the meeting, you could tell were saying, "Okay, what have you got now? What's different about it now?" But it had changed because they were in the process of changing the cable law. It had something to do with passing along the cost of the programming production. Our whole deal changed, and the people in charge at the Journal realized that if we're ever going to do this channel, now is the time. One of the reasons was that they weren't going to be charged for the channel. The whole regulatory issue about passing the expense of the channel charges on would no longer be an impediment to carrying.

All of us left, except the decision-making people. It was two hours later, when somebody came up to me and said, "They decided to go ahead and do the channel." I remember looking at him. I said, "What?" You get so used to having meetings and nobody deciding anything.

Without Jack, I never would have understood the importance of selling. When I say *selling*, I don't mean like trying to sell somebody a car or something. It's more like when you have something, whether it's an idea or a product or whatever, and you want other people to buy into it. Jack showed me very quickly that it's not going to just happen. First, you have to be totally committed to it. You have to be totally knowledgeable, and then you have to take your conviction and show it in the way you present it, in the way you talk about it.

I'd heard about all of that stuff, but I'd never seen anybody who was so effective at doing that and disciplined at going through that process and proving over and over again that it worked. It doesn't work 100 percent of the time, but it can work. If you don't do this, if you don't do it this way, and you're not totally committed to what you're doing, it will never work. You're just wasting your time.

CNN was the first to say, "Okay, we're going to give local cable systems two minutes an hour of air time to sell." I put together a plan to sell local advertising because I was responsible for the budgets for programming. Every year, I'd go in with a budget, and they would cut it. They'd say, "This is a waste of money because we're not going to get the money back."

I put together this plan for our company to sell local ads. The controller at the time was one of those guys who was negative on anything that had to do with money. Automatically his answer was no. Jack came in to the company shortly after that.

Each of us had to sit down and meet with Jack. I didn't know his background, didn't know him at all. I just took my little plans for advertising. Jack said, "Tell me what you're doing." I told him, "I think we could improve or expand it all if we could generate money by selling advertising." He goes, "Advertising. Of course!" I said, "Well, I have this plan here, but the controller says we can't do that." He goes, "Don't you worry about that. What do you know about advertising?"

Jack feels deeply about things. We had a couple of presidents of the cable company. They were what I considered to be cold corporate types. That's not Jack at all. Once he believes in something or a person, he's very committed and supportive.

People say to me, "The reason the Food Network works is . . ." and they always give like this one simple explanation. I look at them and go, "Well, that's one of the fifty-eight reasons, I think, but you're missing a whole lot more."

When you really think about it and look back on it, you really appreciate how complex and complicated these things actually are. It takes a tremendous amount of work by a lot of different people to make anything work. All these other projects I have worked on failed because they didn't have everything the Food Network had. As a result, they just didn't work.

I started a website at the Food Network. The reason we started it was not because I had this big vision for websites. I had fooled around with Prodigy and CompuServe even before we started the Food Network. The Providence Journal put me on a committee to study the future of video text. They called it "video text" at that time in newspapers. We went to this meeting back in the eighties with about fifty people at a hotel in New York.

The main speaker started talking about how the first application for this technology was being done right then in France. A French telephone company wanted to eliminate phone books. They put these little machines in people's houses that were hooked up to their phones. The residents could look up a phone number on them. Somebody asked him, "What does this mean for us?" and the speaker said, "This whole technology is a solution looking for a problem." I always remembered that. When we started the Food Network, I read an article in the *Boston Globe* about MIT working on something called the World Wide Web. I started looking into it.

One of our biggest problems at the Food Network at the time was distributing recipes. We couldn't print cookbooks. The lag time between finishing a show and getting a cookbook ready was way out of synch. The only way we could get recipes out to people was to say, "If you want a copy of the recipe, send in a self-addressed stamped envelope."

That grew so fast and so big that it was on track to cost the network almost a million dollars a year. This is not paying for postage. This is just paying the handling fees of people copying recipes, putting them in envelopes, and sending them out to viewers.

We had a monster on our hands. When I read about the web, I thought that maybe we could put the recipes online. At that time

AOL was emerging. Most people logged on to AOL for their e-mail, but there was also content there. We approached AOL about putting our recipes on there, so we could tell our viewers to go to AOL and get the recipes.

They wanted to charge us big bucks. We said, "No, the hell with that." We tried to figure out how to use the web. I visited a couple of companies in New York, and they wanted to charge us $175,000. One wanted $300,000 to do a website. I'm talking about a website you and I could do in an afternoon now for nothing. That's the kind of money they wanted at that time.

I went back to Reese and said, "The cheapest place we could find is $175,000." He said, "That's crazy. Forget it." Then I went back to Don, our savvy computer guy, who said, "Let me fool around with it more." Don came back and said, "Listen, I found the software. I think I could put one together for $12,000." I really had a lot of faith in Don. He's not the kind of guy to say something like that if he didn't really think it through.

Reese Schonfeld was the first president of the Food Network. I went back to Reese and said, "I think we can do this for, Don says $12,000, maybe $12,500." Reese says, "Let's say $15,000. If he can do it for under $15,000, do it."

We did it, and it became one of the top twenty-five websites within six months. All we were doing was telling people at the end of every show to go to the website to get the recipes. Then we started charging them money if they wanted a self-addressed envelope returned with the recipe. We said, "You can get it for free if you go on our website, or you can get it for $3.00, and we'll send it to you by mail." It blew up. Like 95 percent of people went on the web. We went from 22,000 recipe requests a week by mail down to like a few hundred. That was over a period of a couple of months.

I got really interested in the Internet when I saw how powerful it could be. Before I left the network, we started experimenting with taking little videos of our restaurant chefs and putting them online. You've got to remember, back then it was all dial-up. It was a postage-stamp-sized video. It was a very poor user experience. We got it working, but it just wasn't that great yet.

If You're Lucky Enough to Have Jack Clifford on Your Side, You're Lucky Enough

TRYGVE E. MYHREN

Trygve E. Myhren

Trygve E. Myhren is a former president and board member of the Providence Journal Company. As Jack's boss at the PRJ, he bought into and was supportive of the concept for a twenty-four-hour food network and the acquisition of King Broadcasting. They remain close friends.

I was chairman and CEO of American Television in Communications, which later became Time Warner Cable. I met Jack in marketing and programming arenas. The organization CTAMS (Cable Television Administration and Marketing Society) had an enormous impact on the industry, and Jack was a big player there.

Jack was also a player at the Cable Advertising Bureau, where he was quite influential because he had, of course, broadcast television advertising experience. That wasn't all there was to cable advertising, but it was very applicable to it. Jack had very significant influence on the Cable Advertising Bureau.

Jack was in some ways an outsized character, a big fellow with a bald head, very articulate and smart and experienced. I always thought highly of him.

When I came to the Providence Journal in 1990, a lot of people expected me to clean house, particularly on the cable side.

I had responsibility for everything: cable, broadcasting, the newspapers and magazines, and our early Internet projects.

Jack, of course, was in charge of both broadcasting and cable. Our cable and broadcast operations were of significance but not real big, although either of them alone was bigger than the newspaper. The *Providence Journal* was the heart of the company from a cultural and historical standpoint but not from a financial standpoint.

It was a family culture, and the *Providence Journal* newspaper had won four Pulitzer Prizes. The newspaper was the oldest continuously published daily in the country. The *Hartford Courant* actually started just before the *Providence Journal*, but it went out of business for a while and then was reconstituted. The culture of the company was stodgy and technologically void. It was difficult for Jack, for example, to do things he wanted to do because he didn't have a champion who understood that there was more to communication and media, and there was going to be a lot more than purely newspapers.

We had some other newspapers, but we owned only a minority interest in them. We were not having much influence, and we weren't making any money. I sold them, and that created a little bit of cash. Also the company had been in the cellular business. After I got there, they made a decision to sell cellular, and that created some money as well.

People expected me to go out and put my team together. Jack and I went out for cocktails and dinner and talked in the office a lot. I came to the conclusion that he was the right guy to run that part of the business and that if he was given a little bit more than he had been, things would go even better for the company. In fact, that's exactly what happened.

The economics of the Providence Journal Company were really tied up in cable and broadcasting. That's where the real action was. Not too long after I got there, Jack was very much in favor of buying King Broadcasting in Seattle and maybe getting King Cable. We were able to accomplish both those things, and we got them quite low in the market.

There's this dynamic that occurs in prices of broadcast stations. Broadcast stations run along, and they might be priced at about nine-and-a-half times cash flow. If times are good, advertising revenue is good. Broadcast is all advertising. All of its revenue is advertising. Then for reasons still unknown to any rational person, the multiple paid for a broadcast station goes up, and it can get as high as thirteen or fourteen. If times are bad, advertising is bad, and the multiple might drop down to eight-and-a-half or eight times.

We bought King at about eight and a half. It was a hell of a purchase. Then we were able to convince the Bullitt family, who owned King Broadcasting, that it would be really good if we bought their cable as well, which we did. It really increased the size of our cable business significantly, and it dramatically increased our broadcast business. We did that purchase at the end of '92. It was something Jack and I very much wanted to do. If Jack had wanted to do it and I hadn't been there, it probably wouldn't have happened, just because it was a costly purchase and taking the company away from its newspaper roots.

But by that time Jack and I had formed a cabal. He and I were very much of a mind that the media business was going to change dramatically and that we had to position our company for that. That meant, first, moving away from dependence on newspapers and, second, getting a lot more technologically savvy.

The head guy, Mike Metcalf, was dead by then, having been killed a few years before. He was in some ways a fan of Jack's. Michael Metcalf was more forward thinking than anybody else in that company. Even though he'd come from a newspaper family, he was able to work his way out of that. He believed in things like cellular, which they bought, and was willing to put money into broadcast and cable. Now they hadn't gotten real big, but they had made progress. He and Jack were doing pretty well together. But then, of course, Mike died, and the question was whether he was killed by the Mafia or died of natural causes. I tried to determine that before I came to the company because I didn't particularly want to get murdered either. I had a family to think about it.

The company had been pretty rough on the Mafia. The Mafia was established in North Providence on Federal Hill. The Patriarca family was really the headquarters of the New England Mob. During the time Jack and I were there, the family eventually was forced out of Providence and went up to the Boston area. The Providence Journal had a reasonable amount to do with that, along with obviously the FBI and even the state police, interestingly enough. The police had not been totally infiltrated by the Mafia.

Management was concerned about the money I was spending there. I was on the board. I could listen to the play-by-play. Jack and I worked together to figure out how to short-circuit some of the objections and eventually just get moving. Unless somebody was going to stop us, we were going to get it done. We did, and it was wonderful. It turned out to be a bonanza for the company, and it didn't hurt us either.

That kind of thinking, which positioned the company differently from those companies that had decided to just be primarily in the newspaper business, was very important. It was controversial there because these people had never known anything else. Eventually the economy recovered, and, therefore, so did the multiples. When we sold King some years later, it was worth dramatically more than it had been.

We looked at starting various cable channels. We were convinced that the returns, if you were successful in starting a cable channel, were way beyond what most people understood. We thought it was a worthwhile exercise.

There was a big battle over starting new things. When I came to the company, I made a condition of my taking the job that we'd be willing to invest in cable channels. I had a long session with the executive committee in which two of the members said, "Well, you know, this is like investing in movies. It's boom and bust. It's really not what our company is all about." I said to them, "Look, that's not what this is about. Investing in cable channels really requires that you've done your research. You've figured out what the consumer interest is, and you determine that you can get carriage by other cable operators. If you've got consumer interest and you've got cable companies that will carry your channel, it's not hard to construct a channel that will work. You may get paid by the people who carry you, or you may not. Even if you don't, you're going to have advertising revenues of significance." I took them through the economics.

Well, that was at my hiring. But then here we are, almost a year and a half later, and Jack and I are thinking about this television food network. The latent hostility on the board against doing something like this began to surface, and then it became a bit of a strategic and political battle to make it happen.

Jack and I were absolutely convinced that this had to happen. I had leverage because I was on the board, but Jack was very convincing in his presentations. Eventually we launched the thing, and we had some partners at launch, some other cable companies that came along, like Scripps, for example.

First, let me say that we looked at a medical channel—medical advice and information for consumers. We actually got fairly deep into that before we decided to bow out. But high on our list was the Food Network because if you looked at the advertising categories available that didn't have a cable channel, the biggest one by far was food. It was also, if you looked at the content of magazines—there were still many general-interest magazines around in those days—there was an amazing amount of stuff about food. And if you looked at the sales of books over the previous thirty, forty years, food rose right to the top.

It was in some ways a no-brainer that we would do food. The question was how the hell to do it. How do you do twenty-four hours of food? Jack had a significant role in helping to convince everybody to do it. It ended up being $40 million that we put into it. For a company our size, that was significant.

But we went ahead and did it. I was convinced it was going to work. We had people in the cable industry who actually laughed at us. Chuck Dolan called me up from New York's Cablevision and really laughed. He said, "You screwed it up this time, Trygve." About nine months later, he called up and said, "You know, I've actually started one of these things too, now, and we're going to run you guys out of town. Why don't we get together?" and I said, "No way." A lot of that went around on that channel.

I had other people in the industry who said we'd lost our mind, but they were wrong. They just didn't see it as a workable channel. Who would watch a food network all day? Who would even look in more than just occasionally? Of course, these were all men saying this. Food was of even greater interest to women, although it's surprising how big the male audience for this thing was and is.

It took us a while to really generate much money. For a couple of years, we really struggled. You really had to question yourself. I don't think my doubts ever overcame my enthusiasm. It got close a few times, but it never quite got there.

Jack became the Pied Piper for the Food Network. We would go to cable shows, and Jack, as you may know, cooked chili. He's a connoisseur of chili peppers and the use of chili in foods. One time we had a big party at my house. We invited a number of people from the company and other cable people around New England. The pièce de resistance was Jack's chili. We had lots of cornbread and chili. It was good stuff.

At these massive cable industry shows in Los Angeles, Las Vegas, Chicago, and other locations that held them annually, we'd have a big booth, and Jack would cook chili and also run chili cook-offs between various celebrities. Maybe some CEO of a cable company and some celebrity would have a chili cook-off. People would watch and eat the chili and vote. It was a kick, and Jack was a major celebrity.

He also really operated as CEO of the Food Network. In addition to everything else he was doing, he took that one on. We had a guy who essentially was the chief operating officer, a fellow named Reese Schonfeld who had started CNN with Ted Turner. Reese was a very good start-up guy. He could do things very inexpensively. He understood how to frame programs, but he was a terrible manager. He just ate people alive. Jack had to fire him after a while. That was not an easy time. Jack was really something else during that period. Jack's very outgoing personality and ability to articulate and create excitement really played beautifully during that whole period.

Jack was also a golfer. He used to call himself "the world's greatest putter." Actually he was a very good putter. One time he got into a Pro-Am in Hawaii and ended up getting into the finals. He sank at least three putts over thirty feet. The pro he was playing with went absolutely wild. It was great stuff. "The world's greatest putter."

I used to play with him at the Rhode Island Country Club, which is a very interesting place. We had some great times together there. I look back on that time, and I think of the expectations I had. Some others in the industry had said, "Trygve, you're going to go up to Rhode Island and clean house. I just know you're going to bring in a great team and so on." Of course, the key to my team was Jack, and he was already there.

The Senior Skins Game 1995, third place finishers, Maui, Hawaii, with Jack Nicklaus (center).

Jack was a very good manager. People enjoyed working for him. He could be demanding, but he was also an awful lot of fun, and he knew what he was doing. That was very important. Of course, in those days, he was married to Marguerite, his first wife. I guess you'd call her long-suffering at that point. Jack was into doing his business thing. After Jack retired, they got into ballroom dancing.

After we were in the Food Network for two years, we were still losing a reasonable amount of money. Oftentimes you'd go to these cable industry conventions where you'd have side meetings. We had a side meeting for the Food Network. We're all sitting there at lunch, and this fellow from Continental Cable got up and started saying that he didn't think the channel had a chance in hell to make it. There were people listening to him. It was a key time because not all of those people had signed up with the channel yet. There were others who could drop it because there were a lot of other channels trying to get carriage, and there wasn't enough room. That meeting was real tough.

I got up and said something fairly direct to this fellow, telling him why he was dead wrong. He was either going to be dead wrong, or we were going to look stupid. Then Jack got up and said something articulate and smart. We put the guy to sleep. That was good, but that's the kind of thing that could have just ruined us.

One of the first personalities we hired was Emeril Lagasse. He wasn't a famous chef when we brought him in; he was a nobody. There are a lot of stories about Emeril. The first three times we tried to script him as to how he should do his show, he bombed. We finally said, "To hell with it, just do it your way," and, all of a sudden, he was an instant success.

Robin Leach was a piece of work. We needed somebody who would break through the consumer consciousness. Robin was about what we could afford. We got Robin, and, of course, Robin liked to party. Unfortunately, at a large dinner party, Robin happened to be sitting at our table. He had this real tootie with him, a real tart named Miriam. We had one of our female directors there. She's very prim and proper, as many of our board members and the family members were.

Robin came in and sat down. You could tell he was a little bit tipsy. This gal seemed to be a little tipsy, too. Then she slid under the table. This lady looked at me and looked at Jack and said, "How could you? How could you?"

But Miriam didn't go down there to do a Monica Lewinsky. She went to pass out. It turned out she was totally drunk. She had to get dragged out of there. That was funny.

Twice a year, we had corporate family meetings because a lot of family members were not on the board. That female board member came to that meeting and just read us the riot act. She talked about how disgusting and disgraceful the Food Network was and all these bad things. It was pretty awful. But, you know, even then we laughed our tails off.

We set up this special show for Robin Leach. The deal was that Robin would go out and shop in a grocery store with a starlet. They would then go to her home and cook a meal. We would film the entire thing. I can't remember what the hell we called that show, but it was a good idea. A lot of people were very interested in it. I think Robin saw it as an opportunity to get a lot of these young things into bed.

Food for Thought

BROOKE BAILEY JOHNSON

Brooke Bailey Johnson

Brooke Bailey Johnson is president of the food category for Scripps Networks Interactive, which includes the Food Network, Food Network *magazine, Food. com, and the Cooking Channel. She is the former executive vice president and general manager of the A&E network.*

I met Jack when I was head of programming at A&E, and he was in charge of the cable assets at the Providence Journal. This was back in the day when cable ownership was less consolidated. A&E used to take big cable owners, operators, and whatnot on a trip every year, usually to Europe but different places. Jack and his wife Marguerite went on the trip with us every year. That's how I got to know him. At that time, there was no Food Network.

Jack told me about the Food Network concept: that it was a consortium of newspaper owners who all had food sections at the time, and they thought it would be interesting to make a twenty-four-hour cable network devoted to food. They thought there might be some synergy there, some content-generating opportunities as a result of these newspaper companies having all this food content.

Most people thought at the time, and I was one of them, that this was cutting the pizza awfully thin, that a twenty-four-hour network devoted to food seemed like a real long shot. It was just too niche. It certainly wasn't entertainment television, as we all thought we knew it. I was in the majority of wrong-minded people who didn't get the vision.

I'm going to guess that five years in, I realized they did have something there. There was a rumor that the Food Network was for sale. I remember going to my boss, the CEO at A&E, and saying it was something we ought to look at.

A&E has changed a lot over the years, but at that time we were a bit more of a niche group of networks. The History Channel was pure to history and upscale. A&E was sort of a commercial PBS, again very upscale, family friendly, positive programming. I remember going to my boss and saying that the Food Network sort of fell into that category, and maybe we should take a look at it.

My boss said they gave it away for ten years free. The affiliate contracts were worthless because they weren't being paid. His point was the concern that, if we bought it, the affiliates wouldn't honor the contract because they weren't paying anything. It wasn't quite as shortsighted a comment as it appears, but it was nevertheless not very farsighted.

Another interesting story, I hope this isn't talking out of school, but the guy running the Food Network at the time was Reese Schonfeld. Reese actually had me over to his office. He said he was thinking about leaving and that he could recommend people to be his successor, and would I be interested? At the time I said no because I was happy at A&E. Certainly at this point, I didn't have the vision for how successful the Food Network would be.

It was actually ironic that I became president of the Food Network because when I had an opportunity to run it, I had turned it down some years before. And then fast-forward to ten years ago, when I was looking for a job. I had taken three years off because my kids were in school, and it was time for me to return to work. I tell this story all the time. When I looked at all the networks in New York, there was no question that the one I most wanted to run was the Food Network and that I was deterred only by the fact that someone was already in the job.

But it turned out that Judy Girard, who was that person, ended up hiring me as head of programming, and then she left the Food Network six months later and I became president. I got my wish but through sort of a fluke.

I think really highly of Jack. He's a great guy. And like a lot of those cable pioneers, he's just a real energetic, risk-taking, good dude.

Chapter 6

Afterword about Afterwards

Too Old to Be Young, Too Young to Be Old

**In my element in the kitchen making
Green Chili Pork Stew!**

Ted Turner

I got to know Ted Turner very well because I once ran a TV station, Channel 11, in Atlanta. I met Ted when he was struggling with WTCG. It was Channel 17, which was a UHF independent station with no network affiliation. It had a bunch of old shows, none of which were very exciting. Channel 17 aimed at kids mostly because it was a marketplace other stations just ignored. The station was not doing well, but Ted was dynamic and had dreams of how he could make the station survive.

He invited me to lunch at the Capital City Club. He is about a year or two older than I am, and we were both in our early forties then. We were the only reasonably young people having lunch. All the elderly members were annoyed with Ted's loud voice, but Ted couldn't care less. Ted doesn't talk to you, he shouts at you. Ted said loudly in a deep, heavy, Texas drawl, even though he was from Cincinnati, "I'm going to tell you, Jack. No way are you ever going to beat my station! I'm going to beat you into the ground!" That was his style, and I understood it. Years later, Ted helped create CNN. Reese Schonfeld, the fellow who helped me with the Food Network, was the man behind the idea of CNN. Years before he joined us, Reese had come to see me about CNN when I had a good-sized cable company. I signed the first cable contract to carry CNN in 1980 because I believed that the more programming we had, the more unique we were.

Guess where Ted Turner put CNN's headquarters? In the Capital City Club . . . he bought the whole damn thing. I was there for the cutting of the tape.

He was a tough competitor at times, very tough. He was lecturing me on the fact that he was going to make his WTCG, Channel 17, a national television station. It was going to be seen everywhere on cable. At that point, I was interested in cable but did not understand it very much. I began to get the glimmer of what his idea was and of the communication satellites in orbit. With a relatively modest investment, a television station in Atlanta could send their signal by that satellite and bring it to the whole country. It didn't cost any more to send it to Phoenix than it did to send it next door. You got yourself a transponder on the satellite and away you went. The station was distributed to the home through cable companies. If a cable company had 30,000 subscribers, Ted would be on their service. Ted's station would be in front of 30,000 subscribers delivered at the expense of the cable operator. Ted would get ten or fifteen cents per subscriber for that programming.

We joined the Academy of Television Arts and Sciences and built our own chat room. I saw Ted every week, meeting in New York City for sales pitches. He's a nut. I told him once just to tease him that I was going to add children's programming to our lineup on the ABC station. He went bananas. He thought I was serious, because that was his big thing to make the station better.

Jane Fonda was strong and liberal yet subdued. Ted ran the show when they were together. She was not talkative. She just quietly stood there while he talked. He was the star; she was not. She was beautiful and had one of the greatest figures I've ever seen. She was made of steel, practically. She was so fit! She hardly said a word. She just stood there, posing for Ted.

I was on the executive committee of the cable association. Ted and I would sit together at these meetings. He came back to Massachusetts when I opened two cable systems, and he attended the grand opening. He graduated from Brown University in Providence, and I worked in Providence.

Ted is a good guy with a lot of guts and courage and is pretty smart. He was always good to me; he was always a friend. We might tease and kid each other, but he never snubbed me or passed me over, and he always was friendly toward me, as I was toward him. He is really a crazy sort of guy, but I happen to like him a lot.

He is unique. Maybe he is a genius, I'm not sure. He did things that violated the rules but did them so well that the rules were changed. He made cable television—he really did—with his crazy Channel 17 out of Atlanta. He bought the Braves, which became "America's Team." The cable operators, mostly men, thought carrying Major League Baseball on their cable systems would be helpful, and it was. Ted went out and talked to the individual cable operators like a friend, not like some guy sitting on the top floor of a forty-story building. It was Ted Turner out there giving them a handshake, slapping them on the back, and taking them out to lunch. He sold the idea.

Ted's crazy ideas were interesting to me, but some were illegal. Ted would not give up. He had perseverance. If it was illegal, he did not care, he was going to do it, and he was willing to spend the money on attorneys and all to convince the FCC and everybody else that they could not stop him, and they could not.

MLB was on his back because he was projecting his club into markets that already had MLB teams, like New York City. He didn't give a damn. He just went ahead and did it, and they could not stop him. He made the satellite business work. He actually owned the satellite transponder—not the satellite but the transponder. But he could not use it for the entire twenty-four hours. The rule was that you had to be a common carrier if you had a satellite, so you had to give at least 50 percent of that satellite's use to other people if they wanted it. Well, that would have ruined the whole point for him.

So he sold off the satellite thing to a friend of his, George Taylor, who called it Southern Satellite Systems. George put Turner on and shared the revenue he got from putting Ted Turner on there. Ted now was up there beaming across the country with cable operators who gladly took him. They did not know anything of programming from Andy Griffith to my nose. It was something new and different they could put on and maybe increase penetration of their cable systems into a market. George got paid a fee per subscriber and Ted was paid back by the cable operation that way. That started the whole thing. To this day, I would give Ted Turner credit for the fact that satellite has become a means of broadcast and cable transmission.

Pete Rose

On November 28, 1978, the Providence Journal Company bought its first television station under my persuasion, Channel 17 in Philadelphia. Pete Rose was a free agent. Gene McCurdy, the general manager of Channel 17, who I thought the world of and is one of the reasons I wanted to buy the station, called me on the phone. He said, "Jack, the Phillies have the opportunity to acquire Pete Rose, and they need money." The deal entailed that we would pay them a percentage of the revenue generated by the baseball telecasts and that there was a minimum we would pay. Nevertheless, I said, "Well, what do they want, what's going on?" They said, "They have a chance to get Pete Rose, and I think that's the one condition they need to fill. If we get him in here, we'll have one heck of a ballpark." They had a team. In any case, they desperately wanted Pete Rose. We had always advanced them money through the year until we used up the commission they got from the television station. They didn't have the money to get Pete Rose, and so I went ahead and told Gene to give them the $600,000 we thought we would be paying them for the rest of the year. He did, and they got Pete Rose. The morning paper said we were the Channel 17 team who got Pete Rose. People would jump up when they saw me and say, "You're the guy who got us Pete Rose." It was the best public relations anyone could have. They won the World Series 4–2! The revenue Channel 12 got from the World Series exceeded $750,000. Our ratings went through the roof! That $600,000 was the best $600,000 any human being ever wrote a check for.

Zoology

I went to college and had to take zoology because it was required. Why, I don't know, but my interest was more in liberal arts than in zoology, psychiatry, or anything of that nature. Everyone had to take zoology where I went to school, and the first day of the first class, we were told we were going to have three days of lecture and two days of laboratory. Dr. Henson said we had to be there on time, we had to complete our work, and if we couldn't make it for some reason, we had better have a damn good reason, or he'd flunk us.

And, I thought, *What a guy*. I rather liked that. I was probably a bit more mature than some of the other kids because of some of the jobs I had, and it didn't bother me, so I decided I would do the best I could. I was taught to read before I went to kindergarten, and I would read, read, and read. I read the entire zoology textbook that week—the entire book. I am reasonably good in that although I don't have a photographic memory I do have a substantial memory. I was on top of my game.

The week ended. On Friday afternoon, he asked the class, "Before you go, can anyone name the one-cell parasite that resides in the intestines of horses?" No one raised their hand, so I did. He said, "Mr. Clifford, do you think you can do that?" I said I thought I could. He said, "Stand up. What is it?" I said, "Dr. Henson, it's *Ascaris megalocephala.*" He looked at me sort of strangely, and I thought, *My God, have I made a mistake?* He said, "Everybody else stand up. I want you to give this young man, Mr. Clifford, a standing round of applause. In the twenty-five years I have been teaching this class, he's the first student to give me the correct answer." I loved that man! Guess what I got in that class? That's right, an "A"! And the good thing that came out of it was that if I really believed, if I really worked, I could be as good as anybody else.

Golf

I began playing golf when I was about twelve years old. My parents were moving every few years because they couldn't buy a home. They'd rent them, and then the owner of the home would sell it out from under them. My new friend Norman Sernick who lived across the street was about one year older than I. One day, we were chatting, and he asked if I played golf. I told him I didn't, and he said, "Well, come on, we're going to play." I proceeded to grab my father's sticks (these were out of the '30s; I would say the equivalent of a 5-iron and a putter). We went over to the Mascoutin Pitch and Putt Golf Course. The longest hole was maybe 170 yards. It was a Sunday morning and Norman brought the golf balls.

We heard grumbling behind us from the men who didn't like the idea of these boys interrupting their normal golf. They thought we would be slow, and they were getting pretty tense about it. I thought the best thing I could do was tee them as high as possible and swing as hard as I could. I realized I needed a 9-iron, but all I had was a 5-iron—called a "mashie niblick"—so I swung and hit a perfect shot. It went towering into the air and I watched it as it dropped down toward the green, went right over the pin and, unfortunately, right over to the green. I hit that like a pro and then heard those guys say, "Hey, these kids are all right!"

I played the rest of the day hacking and chopping, but I really fell in love with golf. From that point forward, I started playing every chance I could. At Mascoutin, you could play nine holes for twenty-five cents, and every time I could put the money together, I went over there and played. I played infrequently in college. Western Michigan had a golf course, but I was too busy just getting through school.

I wanted to play more, and television and golf were beginning to come together in the '50s when I got my degree. CBS had a weekly thing called *All Star Golf.* Walter Schwimmer was the creator, and pros would play.

Pro-Am golf tournament with Arnold Palmer in 1993—we won!

Golf had become magical for young executives. Eisenhower loved golf and had become president, and everybody loved Ike. I thought, *Gee, this is the greatest game.* Somehow, I had managed to put together a cheap set of clubs and started playing. I worked nights, so I was off days, and sometimes during the day, I could go golfing. I became fairly good at it. I fell in love with golf, and I still am. Watching golf is like watching grass grow, but playing golf is very exciting and challenging. I eventually became, I think, a fine golfer.

I took many clients golfing. I never once mentioned business with them while on the golf course; we just had fun together. They admired my golf because I played pretty well. I was a 10 handicap. I never got below a 10, but that is high 70s anywhere, so the clients were eager to play with me. I played every Saturday for sure and every late afternoon in summer. Arizona can be very hot in the summer. Golf has been my sport for fifty to sixty years.

Thanks to being in the media business and owning TV stations, I was invited to Hawaii to play in the Pro-Am Seniors Golf Tournament, which included Arnold Palmer, Jack Nicklaus, and a whole group of people who were fine golfers and older but could still play well. The following two days on television, they would show the first nine of the tournament, then the final nine on Sunday, and then give out the awards. Lee Trevino and people like that played. At any rate, I was very fortunate how it all worked out for me. There were four of us, three amateurs and one pro.

Our first pro was Chi Chi Rodriguez, and he was a scream! He was a lot of fun. He got angry at me and said, "You put suntan lotion on and now your hands are slippery! That was a stupid thing to do! Get that off and never do it again!" I got it off and went out and played, and I never played better in my life! The first hole, I made a thirty-foot putt. The second hole I actually hit the ball on the green, a par 3 over the water. I had about a fifteen-foot putt I sank. Now, we are 2 under par. The third hole was a little short. It was as if I cut the corner, some pretty good golfing, and I came up with a pitching wedge and dropped it next to the hole, and I sank that putt! It went like that all day long. We were 17 under par! We made birdie on every hole except one! Chi Chi called me the finest amateur putter he had ever played with. The second nine was with Arnold Palmer, and I did just as well!

We had a big crowd by this time. Everyone was saying, "He's the world's greatest putter" and so on, and with my ego, I loved every second of it! We finished 17 under par and were notified that we won the Pro-Am all the way. I sat with the Schwimmer people who sponsored it, with Arnold Palmer, Chi Chi, and all the broadcasters who did the show. We had a lovely evening, and of course, it didn't hurt my golf. As a matter of fact, if anything, if might have hurt my work, but I usually took a client or someone I wanted to impress. I played golf in Arizona because if you can take the heat in the morning, you can play 365 days per year. Rarely, it rains.

I played with Jack Nicklaus. We did well and won third place in the Pro-Am, the one in Hawaii for the seniors. I had another good day. Jack was exceedingly friendly and helpful. He joked with us and we had fun. We did okay. The other one was Ray Floyd. Ray didn't really want to do it. He was sort of ineffective. I don't know if that's the way he is, but that day we did very well. I think we came in second. His attitude was sort of "let's get this over with." I've had very good luck in those Pro-Ams. The first Pro-Am I ever won was in 1971 at the Phoenix Open, played at the Arizona Country Club. The Phoenix Open is the oldest tournament on the Pro Tour. In the old days, Bob Hope and all the guys from California would come over and play. It's a good, charitable thing. My group, again, consisted of three amateurs and one pro. I can't remember who the pro was, but we won that thing! It's a very nice event and thrilling to be involved with.

Bob Hope and me at a charity golf tournament in Massachusetts, 1982.

Special Events

In the fall of 1975 I was president of WXIA, an ABC affiliate in Atlanta. President Gerald Ford was in Atlanta to discuss economic recovery. I was invited along with twenty-nine other broadcasters from the southeastern United States to have breakfast with President Ford for a private briefing. I had the great privilege of sitting at his table. There were eight to a table, and I chatted with him at great length. I reminded him that I grew up in his hometown of Grand Rapids, Michigan. My high school graduating class of 1951 went to Washington as his guest, and he remembered seeing me. We laughed about the reason he remembered me: I was prematurely balding.

As head of a large broadcasting company, I was invited years later to attend a private meeting with Henry Kissinger, who was serving as President Nixon's secretary of state. His off-the-record presentation to about fifteen broadcasters was quite detailed about world affairs. He specifically spoke of the threat of communism and America's response to it. Following the presentation, I had the honor of speaking to him one on one. I came to believe that he was the most intelligent person in the Nixon administration.

I was fortunate to take advantage of an invitation to observe the one hundredth launch of the space shuttle on October 11, 2000, from Cape Canaveral, Florida. I toured the entire rocket center and the launch facility and met the commander and crew of that historic space event. I sat in a special grandstand about one mile from the launch site and watched the launch just after 6 p.m. The dusk setting made the vivid colors of the rocket launch spectacular. It was one of the most exciting events I had ever seen.

Dick Cavett Music Channel

When we went public with the Providence Journal Company, the underwriters valued the newspaper division at $400 million and my division at $3.2 billion. I suddenly became quite a hero around the Providence Journal Company, as you can imagine. After the success with the Food Network, I was looking for something else to do. My older sister educated me on classical music when I was a small boy because she loved it. I have always loved good classical music; to me, it's the finest music ever written and played. That doesn't necessarily mean everyone feels that way, but a lot of people do. I was on the board of directors of C-SPAN. CSPAN had their Big Yellow Bus, and their booth was next to the Food Network's at a convention in Los Angeles. I wandered over to shake hands with the guys I knew.

We were chatting when this fellow comes over and introduces himself with another chap. Ralph Malvik introduced himself and Linwood Lloyd, the president and general manager of WETA, the public TV broadcast service for Washington D.C. Ralph had helped create the Learning Channel but now was working at WETA on new ventures. They had a radio station that ran all classical music. Ralph, on their behalf, had found out there were hundreds of these contemporary classical music videos. He was able to latch on to them and get the TV rights. The producers at Sony didn't care as long as they got on the air somewhere, because that would encourage record stores to sell the music.

I came up with getting Dick Cavett as the host of this thing because I had seen him do the Detroit Symphony recordings, and I liked him. He's funny. I wanted it to be based on the research we did after that. I wanted a comfortable time for presentation, otherwise it would get too stiff. It was going to be stiff enough if you weren't careful. Dick Cavett agreed to do it. We became buddies, and we paid him some good money. We went to the big convention and showed the tape. A lot of people showed excitement about it, but nobody bought it. We tried and tried, but we couldn't seem to break through. If they took it, it would have been just like the Food Network. It would be on twenty-four hours per day, seven days per week, classical music videos hosted by Dick Cavett.

Research shows that at about age forty, people begin to drift over into the classical music genre. Up until then, they are rock-and-rollers. Not everybody, but the average person. So, the audience really averages out at about fifty years of age. Now, what's good about that? Think about it—the money. Advertisers like Lexus, Mercedes, Tiffany, and Gucci want them. We weren't going to be selling ratings; we were going to be selling demographic relationships.

Dancing

About ten years ago, Marguerite, my first wife, and I danced all over the United States and Europe. In Hawaii, we went to the annual dance championships and had a glorious time. Tony Dovolani was one of the judges. I had met Tony briefly before.

Tony played a small but important role in *Shall We Dance*, the 2004 movie with Richard Gere and Susan Sarandon. He is one of the choreographers with *Dancing With the Stars*. He's a marvelous guy. Through him, I met his manager, who at that time was Gerry Katz. Tony came to Arizona to judge a big dance contest. Afterward I said, "Tony, you have to sign me up for *Dancing With the Stars*. Would you be willing to come to Arizona and be the guest artist for the first "Arizona Dancing With the Stars" for the benefit of the Arizona Kidney Foundation?" He said he would. Of course, we paid him. He came and we raised money for the Kidney Foundation. Over the years, we have raised almost $3 million, and that's not bad. Tony has always kept in touch on this. He was wonderful that first night. He danced with everybody and got this fundraiser off to a hell of a good start.

Gerry and I came up with this idea of teaching people how to dance on TV, but it didn't work. That was around 2005. We charged

**In front of my Cessna Citation
with our ballroom dance troupe in 1984.**

$4.99 to get a complete set of lessons, and nobody, I mean nobody, bought it. Research said they would be interested, but what we found is that people like to watch other people dance, but they don't necessarily want to dance themselves. Most men do not. We had it set up so you could buy individual lessons or a whole set of lessons for a lot less than going to a studio. But it didn't work, and I don't think it ever will.

As a dancer, I was excited when *Dancing With the Stars* originally came on TV. Plus, we already knew Tony, so we were doubly excited. The first time I saw it on TV, I thought it was wonderful! Originally, it was just a show to fill in time before the fall TV season began. It took off like gangbusters and was one of the top-rated programs. Marguerite and I went every year at least once or twice to California as guests of that show, through Tony and Gerry. We would go out to dinner afterward and have a great time.

Backstage they have a series of cubicles for interviews. They're small but lit properly so a guy with a video camera can get a good shot. All of the dancers have their own little slot, where they're interviewed by the press. One night we were standing there watching when Sarah Palin's daughter was on. She had gotten knocked off fairly early. Beverly and I were standing there when this cameraman came rushing over with a reporter and said, "Hi, folks. Can I interview you?" I said we were just there as guests. He said, "Well, aren't you the grandparents of Ms. Palin?" And I said, "No, no we're not."

We talk to the dancers backstage all the time and most are very pleasant. We know most of the professional dancers. When Tony came to Arizona for that first show, he really put us on the map. We were auctioning off a dance with Tony, and this one little girl wanted to dance with him. Her parents paid for it. He went over and treated her so kindly. I mean, he didn't just dance with her, he made her evening. Everybody in that place fell in love with Tony.

These dance contests in Arizona are held in big hotels and ballrooms. You have to pay for each dance. The more dances you do, the better chance you have of winning. They are fairly expensive. For example, at the National Championship held in Las Vegas at the Luxor, I did 108 dances for two days and went out and won every single one of them.

They tell you when you go on the floor what dance you're going to do. We all go out there with our partner, and they may say, "This is going to be the Cha-Cha-Cha, so let's see what you can do." We have to do every dance you can think of—waltz, foxtrot, tango, western two-step, rumba. It's a lot of fun, and I never pay attention to the audience. It's a huge audience, but who cares? They're seated in grandstands all the way around the floor. Fans pay to go to it. On the final night, when they give away all of the awards, we may have five or six hundred people. There has to be one or two going on every week of the year, all over the country.

If you agree to be on *Dancing With the Stars*, you literally commit all of your time. These guys are dancing eight hours per day, five days per week at least. You cannot teach people to do the kind of dancing they're doing by dancing a half hour here and there. We're talking about some pretty tough stuff. Notice how many improve from week to week. By the time they're done, they're nearly professional dancers.

Dance ballroom competition with instructor Yelena Babyuk, 2007.

Mickey Mouse

From the time I was a little boy, I was fascinated with motion pictures. There was no television until I was in high school. My sister, being eleven years older than I, would frequently babysit me. Many times she would take me with her to the movies. Until I was about six or seven, I slept through most of the movie but was still fascinated with it. At age seven, for Christmas I was given a 16mm silent motion picture projector and a box of old Disney cartoons, one of which featured Mickey Mouse. I think that was the beginning of my ultimate career. I would show my movies on a sheet tied on the clothes line in the basement. I would charge the neighborhood kids one or two cents to see the show.

One evening I discovered that the further I moved the projector away from the screen, the larger the picture. The neighbor's house was a white wood-slatted home about thirty feet away from our home. Our kitchen overlooked their living room. One night I set up my projector and aimed it at their house. They were not home at the time. They had two young daughters about my age or younger. I was not aware that Patty, the teenage girl from across the street, was babysitting their youngsters. Patty was quite voluptuous, and I guess she was about sixteen years old.

I turned on the projector, and a giant Mickey Mouse danced across the walls in their living room. Suddenly, Patty leapt up from the couch with her bosoms exposed. She and her boyfriend were dumbfounded by the projection playing on the wall. I quickly turned off the projector and put it away. I hid in my bedroom, hoping no one would discover I was the culprit! Patty today would be well into her 90s, and if she's reading this book, I ask for her forgiveness. Interesting how this one simple machine led to my successful career.

Talk of the Town

Channel 3 in Phoenix ran an afternoon talk show with a socialite hostess named Chris. She interviewed important people in the social swim. I was her alter ego, her Ed McMahon. My job was to open the show and then bring the guests into the studio and introduce them to Chris and the audience. As foolish as it may seem, the floor crew and I decided to have fun with her one day. She was not the brightest bulb in the lamp but very pretty and social.

One afternoon, we made up one of the floor crew to look like a very elderly American Indian. I introduced this man to Chris on the show as the oldest living American Indian chief. Keep in mind that Phoenix was and is surrounded by a number of Indian reservations. Chief Watatumba was the name we came up with. He sat on the couch next to Chris' desk. Chris welcomed him to the show and was taking this thing very seriously. She asked him how he felt. With that he gasped, took his last breath, and fell off the couch onto the floor "dead."

I rushed onto the set and took his pulse. I announced, "Chief Watatumba *was* the oldest living chief!" With that several of our crew grabbed him by the ankles and pulled him across the stage and off the set. The next day, all of us involved with this were called into the general manager's office. Indian tribes surrounding Phoenix were up in arms over this broadcast and were highly critical of Channel 3 for hosting this shenanigan. The general manager wanted to know who was responsible! I have never seen so many fingers pointing in all directions in my life. In exasperation, the general manager, not being able to figure out who was to blame, told us to go back to work. Later he made amends with the Indian tribes.

Jungle Jack

I appeared on a show called *Jungle Jack*. I was Cliff, the Arden Dairy Farm's jungle delivery man. Jack was the owner of a reptile zoo in Mesa, Arizona. The show was on Wednesdays from 6:00 to 6:30 p.m. I was paid a modest talent fee to do this program, but the money was important to my total income. At the time being on television was not a lucrative career. I was paid only $80 a week.

The set was a thatched hut in the jungle. We had dry ice to create a mist. In the background were the haunting sounds of jungle drums. Jack would bring interesting animals on the set each week, and I would interview him about the species. One week,

Jack brought on what he claimed was the world's largest python. It was a huge snake—eighteen feet long. I was horrified at the thought of this reptile being on stage with me. Jack explained to me that I would hold the tail end of the snake. This would prevent the snake from coiling around Jack, who was holding its head. If the snake got loose, it would coil around Jack and crush him. Keep in mind that I was wearing a white Arden Dairy Farm uniform. We stretched the snake out to showcase its eighteen-foot length. Suddenly, the snake decided to crap! A mucous brown liquid spewed out all over my lily white uniform. Of course I couldn't let go of the snake, so I stood there being drenched in snake feces. Jack was unaware of what was happening to me, but the camera was showing it to the entire Arizona market. Jack said, "How are you doing down there, Cliff?" And I answered, "I think you gave me the WRONG END!"

Another incident of note on the *Jungle Jack* show was the night of the rattlesnakes! Jack brought to the set a cage of eighteen rattle snakes. He was going to explain the individuality of each snake and how poisonous each was. The cage was set on a table, and Jack and I stood next to it. He had a gripper to pick up each snake. He pulled the top of the cage to open it. Unfortunately, the stage crew set the cage upside down. When he pulled the cage up, the whole bottom dropped out and all eighteen snakes escaped and slithered everywhere. The floor crew locked their cameras in place and fled the studio. I jumped up on the display of the sponsors' products, and Jack with high boots on, began trying to recapture the snakes. After all was said and done, he managed to retrieve only seventeen of the eighteen snakes. From that day on, we were all frightened to come face to face with the unclaimed snake. We secretly hoped he had escaped outside the studio. The wire services carried the story nationwide showing Jack capturing the snakes in the foreground and yours truly quivering on top of the display of the sponsors' products.

Live Television

It's hard to explain to today's generation that the first TV broadcasts were never taped. All shows were produced live, and there was no opportunity to edit or do outtakes. One of my first experiences involved a show called *Comedy Caravan*. The set was made to look like a circus. I was the barker, who introduced the ringmaster and did the commercial content. Many acts passed through that stage. The permanent cast included Dolly, a scantily clad showgirl, and Bobo the clown. She was known as the "Silver Dollar Girl" because she gave out silver dollars to the children in the audience who asked questions about the show. Dolly was quite young and intriguing. Bobo was obviously smitten with her. As she paraded around nightly, Bobo couldn't take his eyes off her. One evening in the midst of one of my commercial presentations, Dolly's loud voice rang out from behind the set: "Bobo, you pinch my ass one more time and I'm out of here!" The audience was horrified, I was speechless, and the next week the show went off the air.

Cellular Telephone

In the early '80s the FCC announced a new form of personal communication called cellular radio. It was subsequently renamed cellular telephone. I was asked by the Providence Journal Company to look into this idea. The Feds were going to select two companies to serve each marketing area in the United States. The all ready "wire line" got the "A" franchise. The second "B" franchise was to be awarded to companies not connected with existing phone companies; thus a competition began. I set up the Providence Journal Cellular Company. We began identifying markets we wanted to serve and made comprehensive applications costing many thousands of dollars. Many other nontelecommunications entities did the same. The FCC was overwhelmed by the numerous applications. The applicants saw that the Feds were not going forward and choose to negotiate among themselves to settle this logjam.

For example, each of the "B" applicants might have applications in ten markets with a population totaling 3 million. Thus, they had 3 million "pops" to trade. My company wound up being the only applicant for a number of markets through this process. The application process continued beyond our settlements, and when the FCC decided they would accept postcard applications from anybody, all of our expensive applications outside of those we'd settled were thrown out. Thus began the electronic land rush called the cellular lottery. Secretaries, sales reps, and marketing people by the thousands sent in these postcards. Then the FCC drew the winners. The people who won the franchises had no intention of building them; they planned to sell to people like me. Thus, the remaining franchises were purchased by professional communication companies, and a large number of opportunists became very wealthy.

Thanks to our being involved in competitive businesses, we quickly dominated our markets. The phone companies were a bad second place. It became known to the wire line telephone systems that cellular was not just an add-on business but one day could replace the wire line service altogether. Charlotte and Raleigh were two of our markets. To establish our cellular service, we aggressively advertised and sold cellular.

In the midst of the beginning of all this, Hurricane Hugo struck the Carolinas and caused considerable damage, particularly in Charlotte. The wire line service was knocked out, but our cellular operations were in good shape. I instructed our Charlotte cellular management to offer free phones and service to all of the emergency personnel: police, fire, medical, etc. Something like a thousand phones were distributed. When the emergency finally ended, none of the emergency personnel wanted to give the phones back. So, they very quickly signed up as paying customers for our cellular service. I believe this is an example of doing good by doing good.

It became clear to us that as the cellular phone penetrated the market, the monthly usage dropped dramatically. The wire line company in one market could be the non–wire line class "B" operator in another market. We were approached by a number of phone companies interested in buying out our systems. We chose to sell and made a tremendous return on the investment, which we in turn used to purchase King Broadcasting and other ventures.

Cool Guys in Hotlanta

ALBERT E. DOTSON

Albert E.Dotson

Albert E. Dotson Sr. is a successful entrepreneur and civic leader in Atlanta and Miami. Al Dotson and Jack Clifford became close friends and raised significant funds for the Martin Luther King Jr. YMCA in Atlanta.

I first met Jack in Atlanta through his vice president at Channel 11, WXIA-ABC, Larry Lowenstein. I was managing the Sears store and was involved with the Butler Street Y. I was asked to chair the fundraising on their membership campaign, and Larry suggested that we ask Jack to be my co-chair. As part of that, we formed a committee of community volunteers to raise funds for the Y.

Our one stipulation was that it would be a four-week campaign, and we needed to raise over $100,000. Jack and I met with the campaign committee and laid out our program of only four meetings. We would meet every week. If we brought in $25,000, at the end of the four weeks, we'd have our $100,000.

At that time, Maynard Jackson was the mayor of Atlanta. Andy Young was up in Washington. John Lewis had not yet run for Congress. Julian Bond was in the state legislature.

Jack had some apprehensions about us being able to do it. He said, "Are you sure we can do it in four weeks?" I said, "Jack, we can do it!" and he said, "Okay, let's go for it."

We went for it, and the first week was fairly decent. We reached our goal. The second week, it got a little hairy because we did not come up with our twenty-five, and the third week, we were right on it, but we needed to make up what we didn't get the second week. In our meeting, which was an open forum, we started to mention some of the people who had passed through Butler Street

Y, and maybe they'd need to make an investment. We used the analogy of the "bridge" that brought you over because anyone who was someone had gone through the Butler Street Y.

We pulled out some names. The "bridge" was rickety and needed repair. We need for you to step up! Word got out. We were calling people, and, lo and behold, the fourth week, we went over our goal. That was a real treat for the Y.

Our victory dinner was held in the Stadium Club, where the Atlanta Braves played baseball, and our speaker was Earl Graves of *Black Enterprise* magazine. Everyone marveled that we raised that kind of money in such a short time. I want to tell you that Jack hit the phone hard. It was just a unified effort to raise the funds for the Butler Street Y and YMCA.

They took a picture of Jack and me with Earl Graves, but the best picture they took was Jack and I walking out of the Stadium Club locked arm in arm. All you could see was the back of us leaving, him with his bald head. He was bald long before it was popular. I had this big Afro, which was popular then. It was a real telling scene. Here's this Anglo and African American bonded like brothers. We were brothers from different mothers.

That relationship has carried on until this day. When my oldest son was accepted at Dartmouth College in New Hampshire, Jack was at the Providence Journal. I called Jack and said, "Jack, my son is going to Dartmouth. We're going to be coming up to your area." He said, "You're not coming through my area. You're going to stop in my area, and you're going to spend the night with us."

That's what my son Albert and I did. We flew into Boston. I had a childhood friend in Boston, and we went over to Providence and spent the night with Jack and his wife Marguerite.

We kept in touch, and over the years, he'd find me or I would find him because I moved to Miami, and they moved to Arizona. She passed on and went home to glory, but we still stayed in touch. I was overjoyed when I found out he had met his new soul mate. She makes him very happy, and we're happy for them. We talk about how our kids are doing. I'm as proud of his two as he is of my five. If there was ever a true friend in the world, his name would be Jack Clifford.

When I went to Miami, his company bought the local cable station, and we reunited. My new Sears store was in Hialeah, and the station was headquartered in Hialeah. When people saw us meet, they could not believe that we were so close. It was just funny to see their reaction, how we hugged and just made a big fuss over each other. We saw each other again in the early eighties. Now it's 2015, and we're still talking about our love and admiration for each other. We have not seen each other in fifteen years or more. But every time we talk, it's just like yesterday.

When Jack came to Atlanta, we were both at a high level in corporate America. I knew his vice president, who was very personable, and he said, "Al, you think I'm personable. You wait until you meet Jack," and he was right. We hit it off from day one. After Butler Street, I sat on one of their panels at the station doing some things, and it has been a mutual admiration between the two of us. He is so kind and precious.

**Representing ABC in Atlanta during
National Awareness Week for the Disabled
with Paul Raymond (president, CBS; center)
and Don Heald (president, NBC), 1975.**

The Dos and Don'ts of Working With Jack Clifford: Do!

JOHN CRAFT

John Craft

John Craft is a professor of journalism and mass communication at Arizona State University. He is the author of the textbook American Media.

I came to Arizona to teach television. Jack was the general manager of Channel 12. I made a point of meeting all the station people I could, and Jack was a really nice guy.

Then Jack moved to Atlanta, to Sacramento, and eventually to Providence, Rhode Island. I lost track of him over those years. Twelve or fifteen years ago, I was walking down Stafford Hall at ASU and looked in the director's office, and there sits this guy who looked an awful lot like Jack Clifford. I went in and looked, and he said, "I know you" and pointed at me. I pointed at him and said, "I know you, too."

After that, we got together and had lunch. Our wives got together. The four of us would go out to lunch or dinner every once in a while. We really built up a very nice relationship. It started out professional, but we ended up as very good friends.

Back to when I first moved here. I wanted to know all the local professional people so that my students could get jobs. That was basically what I was trying to do, and he was very receptive to talking with me. It was just a good relationship. Jack is an incredibly giving person.

I taught broadcast management at ASU for a long time, and he would come into classes every year and talk about right and wrong in the broadcast management business. I thought that was just wonderful. His background is from roughly the same period of time. He grew up with the same work ethic and the same understanding of what is right and what is wrong.

Bob Schieffer of CBS News, recipient of the Walter Cronkite Award for Excellence in Journalism, 2013 (with my wife Beverly and Phebe Thompson, widow of Ray Thompson, my co-anchor in 1957–58).

One of the stories he tells is back when he was on radio in his college days, basically he was running the night shift, and there was a tornado that came through town. He stayed on the air in that radio station, giving reports and news coming in. He was afraid that the manager of the station, the owner of the station, would be upset. He didn't do what he was supposed to do. Instead he just went all news, getting reports coming in and putting them over the air.

That's what the community station is supposed to do. It's supposed to serve the public. And part of that service certainly is entertainment, and part of it certainly is telling you the best buy on your tires, but a whole lot of it goes into what the community needs to know in order to be safe, prosperous, and happy. Jack understood that from his very first job.

The students loved listening to him because he's so outgoing. That comes from his sales background, which catapulted him into a management role. He is very friendly, outgoing, and could relate to them well, so they understood and related back to him. It was always a highlight of the semester when he came into those management classes and talked about ethical concerns in broadcast management.

I would try to have some classes meet at the TV stations. One year, my students' assignment was to present to Jack an idea of what they would do as managers of the station, and they really took it seriously. They loved that Jack, one of the top broadcast executives in the country, was listening to their presentation. I was happy with how serious they took it. Jack pointed out some of their errors as well as some of their good points, which is a good way to go about doing things. I was always very pleased to have him come in to talk.

Jack is a very important guy in cable television. He was highly respected and one of the innovators of cable television programming. That's an important part of his legacy.

My wife Beverly and I with Robin Roberts at the 2014 Walter Cronkite Award Luncheon, Phoenix, AZ.

On the Road Again

RALPH MALVIK

Ralph Malvik

Ralph Malvik is a cable industry veteran. As vice president of programming, Malvik was part of the small management team that founded the Learning Channel (TLC) in 1980 as one of the first cable channels. In 1991 the Learning Channel was sold to Discovery Communications.

Jack and I were both in the cable industry for quite a while. When we met, I was at WETA Public Broadcasting in Washington. I was one of the founders of the Learning Channel in 1980 and was head of programming there. It's known as TLC now, and they've changed the format dramatically.

In the mid-nineties or so, I went to WETA with an idea for a classical music cable channel because there was nothing else like that. I knew that, like at the beginning of MTV, filmmakers were producing classical music videos, short pieces where the video complemented the music.

While working there in a business development capacity, I wrote the business plan and financial projections. One day, I was at the annual cable convention in Atlanta. I had stopped by the C-SPAN booth, which was actually a bus. Rob Kennedy, who's now the president of C-SPAN, introduced me to Jack.

At that time, our son lived in Prescott, Arizona—about two hours from Scottsdale. My wife and I were planning to visit our son at the end of May. Jack had just retired from the Providence Journal Company and was thinking of doing some consulting. I said, "Can I stop by and see you?"

We flew into Phoenix and then stopped by their house. I met his wife, Marguerite, and explained the whole thing. He was very interested. We said we'd keep in touch. Patty and I drove up to

Prescott, and the next morning, he called me at the hotel and said, "I've already raised a million dollars," which is typical of Jack. He'd gone to a few of his neighbors.

That's how we began our association. He came in as a consultant. The cable industry has changed dramatically since then. At that time, you really needed to get the major cable companies as investors. Time Warner and Comcast were the gatekeepers. In other words, by investing in your concept, they would also make sure you had distribution.

We went around the country and made presentations to pitch the idea. We got a commitment of $10 million from Discovery Communications, and we almost had the final funding from Adelphia Cable in Pennsylvania. It was a handshake deal. We needed about $40 million. Luckily, the Adelphia head honchos went to jail. Usually in that kind of deal, they don't give you the money all at once but in installments. We might have gotten the first $10 million of the $40, but when they went to jail, we would never have received the rest of it, and we would have been up the creek. At that point, with Adelphia's decision, we just didn't have the money to go forward. We folded the company. This process took about two years.

Dancing with the Stars

CLIFF OCHSER

Cliff Ochser

Cliff Ochser has held management positions with Chapman University, the University of California–Irvine, the American Foundation for AIDS research, Arizona State University, and Lowell Observatory. He is the owner of Sedona Stargazing, a Trip Advisor top 10 selection.

I was hired by Lowell Observatory in Flagstaff, Arizona, as a fundraiser. They had been trying to raise money to build this new telescope for about ten years without much success. I was hired to help them with this project because I had twenty years' experience with big capital fundraising projects.

Logically, the first thing I did was to look and see who had already made commitments to the telescope project. There weren't too many—only two! I wanted to visit with the people who saw the vision and made the commitment.

Jack had made the initial contribution to the project, so I called him. It was my first week on the job, and I said, "I want to come visit you. I'm the new guy in town." Of course he was gracious and said, "Absolutely. Come down to Scottsdale and see me."

I was struck by how genuine Jack was, how committed he was, how he saw the vision, and, mostly, how he was one of the few people who actually believed it could be done. I was delighted to see that we had somebody like Jack who saw the vision and really felt like this could get done.

We ended up spending quite a bit of time together. I would go down there to his house a couple of times a month. I really enjoyed Jack and Marguerite both. They ended up becoming friends of mine.

Jack was involved in lots of different things. He was pulled in many, many directions—the symphony and the opera and his scholarships. He was a tough guy to pin down sometimes, but I always felt like Jack and I were kindred spirits, that we were the two people who felt like we could get this accomplished, even in the face of a lot of naysayers.

We started talking about how we might go about a fundraising campaign to raise $30 million. Lowell Observatory was a little $5 million organization. It was going to be quite a challenge for them. But I knew, once I learned about Jack and his background and his sphere of influence and the people he knew, that we'd succeed.

He started coming up with names of people I should go visit and said he would open the doors for those visits. He'd even go with me on some of those visits to introduce the idea of what we were trying to do in building this telescope.

Jack was completely committed to it. He was remarkable. I had worked with lots of different volunteers in different organizations, universities, and other places, but he was most remarkable in his commitment and willingness to actually put his name on the line and make the phone calls and put himself out there.

He introduced me to a number of people who were very helpful. Probably the most significant person was John Hendricks, the founder and chairman of Discovery Communications, owner of the Discovery Channel. They had a long history.

He introduced me to John and set up an appointment for me to go to Bethesda, Maryland, to meet him. Jack was very helpful in coaching me on how to approach the Discovery Channel. It took a couple of years of building a relationship with them and getting them to understand the vision, and Jack was extremely helpful in making that happen. Ultimately, we ended up getting a $10 million commitment from Discovery. We got a $5 million commitment from Mr. Hendricks personally, and a lot of that was because of Jack, because of his relationship and his ability to connect with John.

Jack and I ended up traveling around California and back east, in Washington, D.C., and really became a team. He says it couldn't have happened without me. I say it couldn't have happened without him. Maybe both statements are true, but it's just the fact that we came together to make this happen that was pretty remarkable because nobody really thought it could be done.

Ultimately we ended up getting those lead commitments. Lowell started construction on the telescope in 2002. Ten years later, it was built. The telescope is producing research, and the Discovery Channel is getting content to distribute through their websites and television channels. In fact, they produced a television show on the building of the telescope.

It's the fourth largest telescope in the continental United States. It's a remarkable achievement for such a small institution. A lot of that has to do with Jack's ability to share the vision with people who have the ability to make an impact, and that's what he did.

We've become close friends since then. His is a remarkable story about how you work hard, you treat people well, you have a generous heart, and amazing things will happen. He's a testimony to just what can happen if you have the right perspective and never give up.

Cliff Ochser, fellow astronomer and owner of Sedona Star Gazing, 2015.

From the Land of Ahs

JOHN HENDRICKS

John Henricks

John Hendricks is the founder and CEO of the Discovery Network.

Jack Clifford is one of my oldest and dearest friends in the cable industry. I incorporated the Discovery Channel in '82, but it took three long years to get on satellite. I met Jack Clifford in the fall of 1984 at a cable show in Anaheim. He'd been in the industry for years, not only the cable industry, but prior to that, he was in broadcasting and television. I was like a sponge around Jack because he was a little older than me. He was like my mentor, always willing to help and give his ideas. He was one of the early supporters of Discovery who enabled us to get cable pretty quickly. Jack loved the service.

Jack always loved content. He wasn't just a cable guy distributing other people's content. He was always thinking about ways to improve content. That's what struck me in the early years. Jack was very instrumental in the growth of cable TV.

Whenever there was a meeting of the National Cable Television Association or the Cable Advertising Bureau, I always tried to sit next to Jack. He was just a fountain of knowledge. I was thrilled when he was behind the start of the Food Network. I was as encouraging to him as he was to me when I started Discovery.

I thought he was on the right track with the Food Network. The secret sauce of cable was that we could develop a consistent channel that delivered a content category. In cable, the first big category, of course, was movies, which HBO pioneered. And then it was ESPN with sports and Ted Turner with news. I had the good fortune to do documentaries and nonfiction. Then there were niches like food. The forerunner of that was the Julia Child cooking shows on PBS. Jack had a vision of, again, developing a 24/7 service for people who loved cuisine and loved cooking, not only dining but also preparing food. That was one of the key categories in cable to be developed, and he did it very successfully.

Jack always struck me as a person who's very curious. What I've observed in life is that people who are curious are problem solvers. They tend to be successful in business. He was very curious, not only about the cable business but just in general. Years later, after I met Jack, I was on the board of Lowell Observatory, and we were looking to recruit new board members. Someone said, "We love to have curious people in business." Jack's name immediately came to mind.

I just suspected that he probably had a curiosity for astronomy. I told the group there was someone who actually lived right there in Arizona, probably a couple of hours' drive from Flagstaff and Lowell Observatory. I called Jack. I didn't know he had an observatory of his own! He was an amateur astronomer. It was just a perfect backdrop. He readily agreed to join the board. He's been of great service to Lowell Observatory through the years. I was fortunate to make that introduction, and I'm glad that I did.

Telescopic photo of comet taken by John Hendricks, founder and CEO of the Discovery Networks.

Sometimes God Just Hands You One

BEVERLY CLLIFFORD

Beverly Clifford

Beverly Clifford is the wife of five years to Jack Clifford and mother to Brian Dorsey, Nicole Jennings, and Michele Richter. She taught sixth grade for thirty-five years for the South Bay Union School District, in Imperial Beach, California.

I was separated from my husband in January 2005, and, through a divorce, still supporting my twin daughters through nursing school while my son was abroad teaching English in Barcelona and Daegu, South Korea. In the interim before I met Jack, I certainly wasn't interested in remarrying because I had been married thirty-four years. I just didn't see it coming. I was blindsided. As a Catholic, I knew divorce was a no-no.

I was seeing a therapist, and I found myself at the Catholic church in Coronado, where I ended up taking a class called New Paths. It basically saved my life and renewed my spirit in Christ and religion. I was going to daily Mass and really searching my soul to find my place.

In the summer of 2008 I was meeting all these people from Arizona, through my friends Cheryl and Ira Gaines. Cheryl and Ira knew Jack and me, even though we didn't know each other. They always had a ticket to everything. In fact, they had five tickets, one for Cheryl, one for Ira, one for Cheryl's mother, and two extras to invite couples from Phoenix. They had tickets for Padres games, the symphony, concerts, the theater, whatever.

They gave me the third ticket on the night I met Jack because Cheryl's mother was in a horrific car accident. We were at the San Diego Symphony Summer Pops on the Embarcadero at a pre-event dinner for the sponsors, which Cheryl and Ira were, and the couple they had invited that day was Jack Clifford and his date, a prominent socialite from Phoenix.

As I was sitting there, Cheryl said to me, "Do you know who Jack Clifford is?" I told her I didn't. She told me that he was a ballroom dancer, and I jokingly said I should have paid attention to my children's ballroom dance teacher when they were in sixth grade and took ballroom dancing. Jack overheard me and said, "Well, let me show you a few steps."

He took me in his arms next to the concert stage before the symphony and started showing me how to do the rumba, but I need to see things first, and he was saying, "Quick, quick, slow, and put your right foot here and there," and I'm looking down at my feet. He said, "No, no, no, darling, look into my eyes." And then I looked up into those baby blues, and the rest is history. I was sort of uncomfortable because I thought, *My god, he's got this date here, and he's making the moves on me.* I thanked him for showing me the dance and sat down.

Cheryl nudged me again and said, "Do you know who Jack Clifford is?" I said, "Yeah, a ballroom dancer," and she said, "No, he created the Food Network." I was stunned and just about a puddle on the floor, and I said, "Oh, my gosh. That's quite something."

We attended the concert, and, afterward, Cheryl said, "Let's walk Jack and his date back to their car." I assumed they were parked in the preferred parking for the concert season ticket holders. Oh, no. He had a town car and limo driver. I expressed that I enjoyed meeting him. Jack put his date in the limo, and he turned to me with his finger like a gun. He went *click,* and he winked at me. I thought, *Oh, a nice guy.* I didn't think anything of it. Then I went into the bowels of the convention center to retrieve my car from the $7 parking garage and went home.

The next day, Ira called and said, "Jack Clifford wants to know if you'll go on a date with him." I said, "Now, wait a minute. I'm not one of these people who jumps into relationships where somebody else is involved." He said, "Oh, no, no, no, she was just a ballroom dance date. Jack lost his wife a couple of years ago, he loves to dance, and it's hard for him to find partners." I thought about it and thought about it. I said, "Sure. What do I have to lose?"

He invited me that Labor Day, the next week, to the beach. That was quite intimidating, getting in a bathing suit on your first date, but we sat on the beach for several hours and talked. We went out to dinner in Coronado that night and hit it off very well, but it was very platonic. There was nothing romantic about it. I learned a lot about Jack and all of the things he's involved in. And, of course, my little world was consumed with being a teacher and getting my girls through nursing school.

During dinner, he extended his arm across the table, and I held his hand. He said, "What are your concerns about a relationship between the two of us?" and I said, "Oh, Jack, you come from a different world than I have ever even known."

I believe he thought I was going to say the difference in our age because there are nineteen years between us. I said, "Age is just a number. The thing for me is that I don't know if I can fit into this world of balls and galas and the things you're accustomed to." He said, "Oh, no, no. I come from a lower-middle-class background. My father was a detective on the railroads. My mother was a homemaker. We never owned our own home; we always rented. My mother was smart enough to always rent in school districts that offered a good education." Of course, he told me the story about Elmo Wierenga and how he had encouraged him to go to school, along with the mentoring of his sister.

So that was our date. I'd gone back to school that September, and Jack went back to Phoenix, where he lived. He had a home in Coronado, his family home, but they only spent the summers there. Apparently Marguerite had bought that home because she wanted somewhere to get out of the summer heat in Phoenix, but, unfortunately, she only was able to enjoy that house for one summer before she passed away. Jack told me the next time he'd be back in Coronado would be for Christmas.

At Christmastime, I was taking decorations down and had some goodies left over. I thought, just as a shot in the dark, just as a friend, I'll call Jack and see how he's doing. I think the catalyst was my friend Leigh's party the next day for New Year's Day. She had come down with the flu, and she called me and said, "What am I going to do, Bev? I've got this big party planned for tomorrow, and I've got the flu." I said, "Is there anybody to help you?" and she said no. I said, "Just hold on."

I never went to Coronado, maybe only once or twice in the summer to go to the beach. I said, "I'll bring you some Gatorade and some medicine and stuff so you can get straightened out, hopefully by tomorrow." Then I thought, *Oh, Jack's in Coronado. Maybe he's over there*, so I called him as well.

Beverly and I at a Fred Astaire Dance competition, Scottsdale, Arizona, 2009.

When I called, he said, "Oh, no, honey, I'm back in Phoenix preparing to be the master of ceremonies for the Symphony Ball on New Year's Eve." He said, "But my family's there. Why don't you go over? I'm sure they'll enjoy seeing you." I had already met Lori, his daughter-in-law, his son Jay's wife. So I went over.

I went in and chit-chatted. I met his daughter from Baltimore, Kristin, and all the grandkids. I gave them some goodies I had baked and left after about a half hour. I really thought that was the end of it. Jack called me the next day after he had hosted the Symphony Ball and said how nice it was of me to do that. He told me Lori said, "Now, Jack, that's the kind of person you should be dating." Apparently, the socialites he had taken an interest in—or, I should say, the other way around—were not liked by the family. So they saw me as sort of a down-to-earth kind of a person.

Jack was back in San Diego for his ballroom dance channel business with Jerry Katz and Tony Dovolani in January. He said, "Will you go out with me again?" That's when I met up with him the second time. I had just returned from an ethnic wedding in Slovakia and was sharing some pictures of the wedding traditions. We were at the Boathouse in Coronado, talking and laughing together. Both of us were quite animated. Jack is always bantering back and forth with the wait staff and the people around us because he's such a people person.

As we were enjoying the evening together, some magic dust came down from the sky, and he turned to me and I turned to him. We looked at each other, and he kissed me right in the restaurant. That's sort of what started our romantic relationship. That was in January 2009. We were engaged in September 2009 and married in July 2010.

When we first became romantically inclined, Jack wanted to marry right away, like after four months together. He said, "That's it. I know this is it." I knew, too, that he was the one for me, but I just needed to get my girls through nursing school. I needed to finish up my teaching career, and I knew from taking these New Paths classes in Coronado that probably 70 percent of second marriages don't make it because of family problems, whether it's children or blending families together. I said, "You know, Jack, we really need to have a long engagement and make sure this is right for our kids, that they get along well together and accept us as a couple."

The whole next year Jack and I made an effort for both of our families to get to know one another and spend time together. We flew my children to Tucson where Jay and his family live. Lori, Jay's wife, arranged for us all to see a Christmas show. Both families came to my house in Chula Vista for dinners. We all congregated at the Clifford house in Coronado for birthdays, Easter dinner, and so on. Everyone got along, and we became very comfortable with one another. That's when I knew it was going to work for both of us.

We took our sixth graders to the Cuyamaca Mountains, about an hour and a half out of San Diego, for science camp. The kids went for a week, and the teachers accompanied them as chaperones. I was there when Jack called me from Arizona. He said, "I'm coming over for the weekend. Would you mind going with me to Santa Anita?" What ran through my mind is, *Oh, my gosh, this man is a gambler. He's going to place bets on horses, and he's coming all the way over here to do that.* But he explained that he owned a horse that was going to be running that weekend. He said, "I need to file the papers, or the horse will not be able to run." So I agreed, but the thought sticking in my head was, *What do I have to wear?* When I asked Jack, he said, "Oh, you know, a nice cocktail dress," and here I am in my dusty jeans at camp.

I left there on Friday, came home, and frantically rummaged through my closet thinking, *Oh, my gosh, I don't own a cocktail dress*, until I found something that would suffice, but I had no shoes. I ran up to Payless shoe store, picked out a pair of shoes, came home, and realized they were a little bit too big. But I figured I just had to go with them, and off I went to pick up Jack in Coronado, and we drove to Santa Anita.

Rollin Baugh, his horse manager, and his wife Bonnie met us at the Turf Club valet parking. That was a whole new situation for me. I had never valeted my car before. They walked with us with me clopping in my new heels that didn't fit through these chandelier-lit lounges with women dripping in jewels. I just felt so out of place.

Bonnie said, "Rollin and Jack need to go file these papers, and I'll take you to your table." We were up in the Turf Club at a cloth-covered table right on the finish line. As Bonnie escorted us to the table, I saw there was already a gentleman seated at the table with his back toward us. I'm standing there with my water bottle from Ralph's grocery store. She said, "I'd like you to meet Alex." I extended my hand, looked down, and, oh, my gosh, it's Alex Trebek. I almost dropped down to my knees. I mean, what do you say to Alex Trebek? Bonnie said, "Can I get you anything?" I said, "Oh, maybe a glass of ice for my water." The whole time she was gone, I was shaking, thinking, "I'm here with Alex Trebek. I've never met a celebrity face to face like this. How do you do small talk with Alex Trebek? I'll take Geography for $200?" It turned out that Jack co-owned the horse Lemon Chiffon with Alex Trebek.

At the early age of fifty-seven, I retired from my teaching career. I can still remember walking through my classroom that last September, and I had gotten my first docucam, which is basically a camera that projects up on the screen. Up until then, I had to run thermofaxes and transparencies for the overhead projector. I knew that with this new docucam, the kids were going to see my engagement ring, and it was going to be the talk of the town.

I had been with the kids for probably about a month when I said, "I just wanted to tell you that you will be a very special class to me because you will be my last." There was sort of a gasp. I said, "I'm engaged to be married at the end of the school year so this will be my last year as a teacher."

That had been my thirty-fifth year. The girls were all goo-goo eyed and thought it was so wonderful—"Ms. Dorsey, we're so happy for you!" The boys were sort of scuttling down behind their desks peering at me with suspicious eyes, like, "What are you talking about?"

At the end of the day, I was walking my class down to the front of the school, and little Ramses pulled on my shirt sleeve and said, "You're getting married?" I said, "Yes, Ramses, I'm getting married." He looked at me questioningly and said, "Are you glad for it?" Jack always said I should write a book about teaching and all the little sayings the kids came up with. He said I should title it *Are You Glad for It?*

We were married the next year. It was quite a time getting adjusted because we moved from San Diego full time over to Phoenix, except for the summer, when we came back to Coronado. At that time, my girls had graduated from nursing school and became RNs. My son Brian began to pursue a teaching career after teaching abroad for a couple of years. Everything seemed to have come to fruition, all the things I had wanted for my children, and now I had met my Prince Charming, and a whole new world was opening up.

I was just so nervous and out of place. Bonnie came back with the glass and put it on the table. As I was trying to make small talk with Alex, I thought I was pouring the water in the glass, but I was actually pouring it all over the table. I was just like Eliza Doolittle, a real mess. Jack came back, laughed it off, and had a nice luncheon with Alex Trebek, even getting his picture taken with Trebek.

One time we were at a Christmas party, and Jack said, "I want you to meet Rose Mofford. Rose was the first female governor of Arizona." Rose was probably in her eighties then and had silver-coiffed French twist hair. She was sitting regally, and Jack marched me up to her and said, "I'd like you to meet my wife, Beverly Clifford." She had this stunned look on her face, smirked at me, and said, "You're the one?" I said, "Yes, I'm Jack's wife, Beverly." She said, "I've been after Jack all these years, and you're the one who got him?" I said, "Oh, it's nice to meet you, Governor Mofford," and I sort of backed away. But she did that to me on another occasion, too.

I also met Justice Sandra Day O'Connor through a fund-raiser, and I had a really good chat with her about sixth-grade students. I told her I was very concerned about No Child Left Behind and the fact that children were not getting their civics and their history and their sciences because all the focus was on math and reading and teaching to the test. She said, "I want your class to log on to the computers in the classroom. I have a website for your children that will help them with civics." That was really special, and I did do that with my class, which enhanced their civics learning.

My family, 2009: Jack James, grandson; Peter Van Houten, son-in-law; Robin Van Houten, grandson; me, Kristin Van Houten, daughter; Lori Clifford, daughter-in-law; Sarah Clifford, granddaughter; Jack Jay Clifford, my son.

That's just a little snapshot of people who have come into my life. Never in my wildest dreams would I have thought I would have a chance to meet a Supreme Court justice, or governor, or, gosh, Alex Trebek. It's been quite a ride with Jack, and every day is a new day. Every day is exciting. Every day he wakes up with a smile on his face and plans our day with so much enthusiasm, it's just so much fun.

He's an accomplished baker. Yesterday, he made hamburger buns. He taught bread baking for about seven years at the community college in Rhode Island, and he's taken cooking classes internationally. He's quite an accomplished cook, and he just loves making his own pickles. One of his favorite foods is eggplant parmesan. We have lots of fun in the kitchen whipping up the things we both enjoy. We are very compatible in that respect. We both love cooking, entertaining, and of course our family and friends.

Blended family, 2009: stepson, Brian Dorsey, stepdaughters, Nicole Jennings, Michele Richter, my new bride, Beverly, me, my daughter, Kristin Van Houten, and my son, Jack Jay Clifford.

It's just been so much fun to be married to Jack. I always tell everyone that I taught sixth grade for thirty-five years in preparation for marrying Jack because he's always into mischief. I call him Mr. Gadget because he has pantries, cabinets, and garages full of gadgets. He has juicers and slicers and Ninjas and George Foremans and ice-cream makers. Every time we go to a cooking store, he's like a kid in a candy store.

I can especially remember going into Bed Bath & Beyond, which is like Disneyland to him. I had turned to do something, and when I turned around, he had the whole cart filled to the top with things he thought he needed for the kitchen. And, you know, you can only put so many things in a kitchen. The overflow was always the garage. He had this Ninja in the cart, and I said, "Jack, you have a Cuisinart. You have a blender. You have choppers and all these other kinds of things that whirl and chop and mince and shred and all that." I said, "Why do you need one more thing like that?" Like a little boy, he put his head down and sheepishly put it back.

Well, I could see how it broke his heart and how much he really wanted that. It was early December. On Christmas morning, guess what Jack got? I had snuck back, gotten the Ninja, and wrapped it up. He was just overjoyed, but that's his spirit. He's a little boy at heart. Everything is bright and shiny and new. He puts his hands in so many things, from ballroom dancing, to classical music, to opera, symphony, cooking, and horse racing. He has a voracious appetite to learn.

I really do believe that Jack is a genius. He whizzes through books; maybe every two or three days, he's read a book. He just consumes them, and he's able to talk articulately about whatever he's read. He's fascinated with astronomy. Of course, he's on the board of the Lowell Observatory. It's just wonderful to see his excitement and how he gets other people motivated.

As a Catholic, I would, of course, go to church every Sunday. Jack asked to go with me, and I said, "You know, Jack, don't go to church to please me. I don't know what your beliefs are." This was in the early stages of our dating, and he said, "No, I really would like to go." He shared with me that he and Marguerite had gone to the Franciscan Renewal Center, also known as the Casa, in Scottsdale on occasion because it was close to their home.

We went to church together. As I said, my faith was renewed after my husband left. Our pastor, Father Pat Mulcahy, was just so wonderful with both Jack and me. He had counseled me during some hard times and saw how happy I was with Jack. Jack announced one day that he wanted to become a Catholic. My first reaction was, "Jack, please don't do this on my account or because you think we need to be married in the Catholic Church." He said, "No, no, no, I see something in you that I want." He said, "I see that deep faith, and I want to learn."

God bless him, he took RCIA (Rite of Christian Initiation of Adults) classes in Scottsdale and Coronado. When we were dating that whole last year I was teaching, he was flying back and forth almost every other weekend and flying me to Scottsdale or Phoenix in between. On Easter in 2010, right before we got married, he received his confirmation and his first communion in front of the congregation at the 9:00 Mass. It was quite joyful for me and for him.

A few months later on July 17, 2010, my parents, Anne and Joe Skrincosky, walked me down the aisle at Corpus Christi Catholic

Parish to be joined with Jack in matrimony by Father Pat. We were surrounded by our families and dearest friends. At the wedding reception in Coronado, Jack had his ballroom choreographer design a dance just for us. The music was "Make Someone Happy" by Jimmy Durante. Jack's motto is to always make someone happy; to always be friendly, engaging, and smiling. Throughout the last five years, we have attended church weekly and are very committed to our faith. We pray together, laugh together, and cry together. All of our joy we attribute to our faith in Jesus Christ.

About Jack Clifford

Jack Carl Clifford was born to Pauline Arndt and Jack Charles Clifford in Gary, Indiana, on September 13, 1933. Clifford graduated from Ottawa Hills High School in Grand Rapids, Michigan, in 1951. He attended Grand Rapids Community College and graduated from Western Michigan University in Kalamazoo, Michigan, in 1955. He helped create the radio station WIDR on the campus of Western, which led to another disc jockey job at WKMI in Kalamazoo to help support tuition costs. On a visit to his sister's home in Phoenix, he applied for a job at KTVK (ABC) and worked as a sportscaster and advertising salesman from 1957 to 1962. Jack married Marguerite Seeds on October 24, 1958. He then went to KTAR-TV (NBC) in the summer of 1962 as a sales representative. Son Jay was born on August 30, 1963, and daughter Kristin on October 21, 1965. In 1968 Clifford was made V.P. of sales, then in 1970 rose to president of KTAR and general manager. In 1974 he moved to Atlanta to assume the president and general manager position at WXIA-TV (ABC). He left for Sacramento in 1976 to be the general sales manager for KXTV (CBS). He was recruited to Providence, Rhode Island, in 1977 to become V.P. of Providence Newspaper Corporation, to run all non-newspaper operations: cellular telephone, radio, broadcast television, and cable TV. He rose to be executive vice president of the Providence Journal, which he took public in 1997. During his tenure at the Providence Journal, he created the Food Network, America's Health Network, and Northwest Cable News. Clifford retired to Phoenix, Arizona, in 1997 and remains a media consultant. He is a board member of Lowell Observatory, on the Endowment Board of Arizona State University's Walter Cronkite School of Journalism, and a former executive board member of the Arizona Opera and Phoenix Symphony. Clifford is a member of the World Presidents' Organization. Jack currently resides in southern California with his wife Beverly.

Other Books by Rich Wolfe

For Cardinals Fans Only—Volume I
Remembering Jack Buck
I Remember Harry Caray
Ron Santo, A Perfect 10
Jeremy Lin, The Asian Sensation
For Cubs Fans Only
For Cubs Fans Only—Volume II
For Notre Dame Fans Only—
   The New Saturday Bible
Da Coach (Mike Ditka)
Tim Russert, We Heartily Knew Ye
For Packers Fans Only
For Hawkeye Fans Only
I Love It, I Love It, I Love It (with Jim Zabel, Iowa announcer)
Oh, What a Knight (Bob Knight)
There's No Expiration Date on Dreams (Tom Brady)
He Graduated Life with Honors and No Regrets (Pat Tillman)
Take This Job and Love It (Jon Gruden)
Remembering Harry Kalas
Been There, Shoulda Done That (John Daly)
And the Last Shall Be First (Kurt Warner)
Sports Fans Who Made Headlines
Fandemonium
Remembering Dale Earnhardt
I Saw It On the Radio (Vin Scully)
The Real McCoy (Al McCoy, Phoenix Suns announcer)
Personal Foul (With Tim Donaghy, former NBA referee)

For Yankee Fans Only	*For South Carolina Fans Only*
For Red Sox Fans Only	*For Clemson Fans Only*
For Browns Fans Only	*For Oklahoma Fans Only*
For Mets Fans Only	*For Yankee Fans Only—Volume II*
For Bronco Fans Only	*For Mizzou Fans Only*
For Michigan Fans Only	*For Kansas City Chiefs Fans Only*
For Milwaukee Braves Fans Only	*For K-State Fans Only*
For Nebraska Fans Only	*For KU Fans Only (Kansas)*
For Buckeye Fans Only	*For Phillies Fans Only*
For Georgia Bulldog Fans Only	

All books are the same size, format and price.
Questions or to order? Contact the author directly at 602-738-5889.